D1476193

What's in This Book?

This 30-unit book contains strategies and practice for learning 450 spelling words.

Each unit contains:

- a list of 15 spelling words
- two sentences for dictation
- four activity pages for practicing the spelling words

Words on the spelling lists were selected from:

- a list of the 400 most commonly used words in English
- words frequently misspelled by third-graders
- words with common phonetic elements
- words changed by adding prefixes and suffixes and by forming compound words and contractions

Additional resources:

- "How to Study" chart
- "Spelling Strategies" chart
- forms for testing and recordkeeping

EMC 2707

Evan-Moor®
EDUCATIONAL PUBLISHERS
Helping Children Learn since 1979

Author: Jo Ellen Moore
Editor: Leslie Sorg
Copy Editor: Cathy Harber
Illustrator: Jim Palmer
Desktop: Jia-Fang Eubanks
                 Yuki Meyer

Contents

Teaching the Weekly Unit

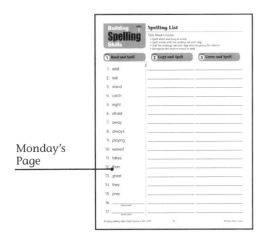

Monday's
Page

Strengthening Students' Spelling Skills

Spelling Strategies
Page 6

How to Study
Your List
Page 7

At the beginning of the year, reproduce pages 6 and 7 for each student or on an overhead transparency. Review the general steps and strategies, encouraging students to apply them throughout the year.

Monday

Allot ample class time each Monday for introducing the spelling list and having students complete the first page of the unit.

Introducing the Week's Words

Give each student the spelling list for the week. Here are ways to introduce the words:

- Call attention to important consistencies noted in "This Week's Focus," such as a phonetic or structural element. For example, say: *As we read this week's spelling list, notice that all the words have the same vowel sound.*

- Read each word aloud and have students repeat it.

- Provide a model sentence using the word. Have several students give their own sentences.

- If desired, add "bonus words" based on the needs of your class. These may be high-utility words or words that the class is encountering in curricular studies.

Writing the Words

After introducing the words, have students study and write the words on the first page of the unit, following these steps:

Step 1: Read and Spell
Have students read the word and spell it aloud.

Step 2: Copy and Spell
Tell students to copy the word onto the first blank line and spell it again, touching each letter as it is spoken.

Step 3: Cover and Spell
Have students fold the paper along the fold line to cover the spelling words so that only the last column shows. Then have students write the word from memory.

Step 4: Uncover and Check
Tell students to open the paper and check the spelling. Students should touch each letter of the word as they spell it aloud.

Home Connection

Send home a copy of the Parent Letter (page 145) and the Take-Home Spelling List for the week (pages 10–19).

Tuesday   Visual Memory Activities

Have students complete the activities on the second page of the unit. Depending on students' abilities, these activities may be completed as a group or independently.

Wednesday   Word Meaning and Dictation

Have students complete the Word Meaning activity on the third page of the unit. Then use the dictation sentences on pages 8 and 9 to guide students through "My Spelling Dictation." Follow these steps:

1. Ask students to listen to the complete sentence as you read it.

2. Say the sentence in phrases, repeating each phrase one time clearly. Have students repeat the phrase.

3. Wait as students write the phrase.

4. When the whole sentence has been written, read it again, having students touch each word as you say it.

Thursday   Word Study Activities

Have students complete the activities on the fourth page. Depending on students' abilities, these activities may be completed as a group or independently.

Friday   Weekly Test

Friday provides students the chance to take the final test and to retake the dictation they did on Wednesday. A reproducible test form is provided on page 142. After the test, students can record their score on the "My Spelling Record" form (page 141).

Tuesday's Page

Wednesday's Page

Thursday's Page

Friday's Page

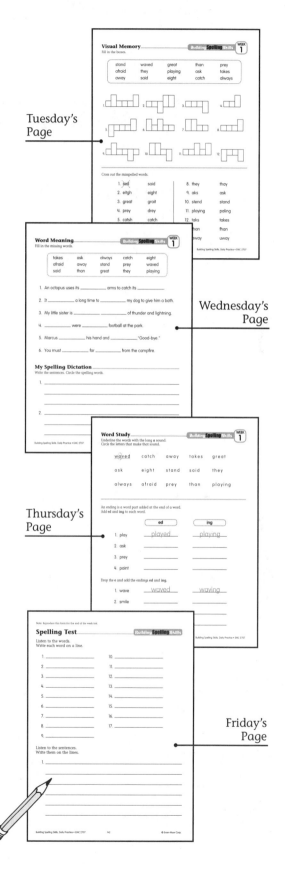

Spelling Strategies

Say a word correctly.

- Don't leave out or mispronounce sounds.
- Write the sounds in the correct order.

Think about what the word looks like.

- Think about how the spelling pattern looks.
- Write it, look at it, and decide if it looks correct.

Look for small words in spelling words.

- spin—**pin**, **in**
- cupcake—**cup**, **cake**

Look at syllables in spelling words.

- Spell the word one syllable at a time.
  remember—**re** • **mem** • **ber**

Use rhyming words to help spell a word.

- If you can spell **book**, you can spell **look**.

Use rules for adding endings.

- Drop silent **e** before adding a suffix.
- Double the final consonant before adding a suffix.
- Change the final **y** to **i** and add **es**.

These strategies help me become a better speller!

6

How to Study Your List

❶ Read and Spell

❷ Copy and Spell

❸ Cover and Spell

❹ Uncover and Check

Good for me!

Sentences for Dictation

There are two dictation sentences for each spelling list. Space for sentence dictation is provided on Wednesday of each week and on Friday's test form (page 142).

- Ask students to listen to the complete sentence as you read it.
- Have students repeat the sentence.
- Read the sentence in phrases, repeating each phrase one time clearly.
- Have students repeat the phrase.
- Allow time for students to write the phrase.
- Read the sentence again, having students touch each word as you say it.

Week Dictation Sentences

1   Were **they always playing** that **great** game?
Jay is **afraid** of things with **eight** legs.

2   Has **she seen** the **sea very many** times?
I **believe** I **left** my lunch **between** those seats.

3   Don't **swim while** the shark is close by.
Why did you shine that **light** in **my eye**?

4   Will your **pocket hold most** of the toy **rockets**?
The king **often** sat on his gold **throne**.

5   **Touch** the **cute**, **young** kitten **under** its chin.
Carlos invented a **new fuel** for **humans** to **use**.

6   The wind **blew** the **blue** kite **above** the trees.
Do you **know** where you will **live** when you **move**?

7   Will the wind **carry** my **pretty balloon off** to **Mississippi**?
Is the artist **willing** to draw a **different pattern**?

8   The note he **received** told who is **getting** the prize.
Are you **coming** to the **swimming** party I'm **having**?

9   The **price** of **uniforms usually stayed** the same.
Her **niece tried** to **float** an ice **cube**.

10   The **teacher** and her **children** went **everywhere together**.
Where do you **think** we need to **search** for it?

11   **Everyone** came to school **without** their **homework today**.
Was **everybody** scared by the **earthquake**?

12   That **tough** kid **called** the **small** boy an **awful** name.
Bob **brought** his **strongest** rope **along** on our camping trip.

13   The **ladies cried** when the **story** was **finally** over.
My **family** gave me **toys** and **shoes** as a **surprise**.

Week Dictation Sentences

14 Is it **true** that the **school** has **good food**?
    Maggie **chewed** on **cookies** until she was **full**.

15 The **boy joined** his dad for a **voyage** across the sea.
    His **choice** was **oysters** and **chocolate** pudding for dinner.

16 **I'm** sure **we're** going where **they're** going.
    The clock **doesn't** work, so **they're** always late.

17 You **should follow** that **group** to the old **house**.
    My **cousin** ran **around town** until she **found** her dog.

18 Did **April's** pet rabbit have **those tiny white babies**?
    Pat **raised** the flag **over** her head.

19 I'm too **tired** to **read** the book **again**.
    Does some of the **money** need to be **given** to Mother?

20 **Clean** up the spilled **cereal** and put it in the **carton**.
    Could the **guards** save the **city** from **danger**?

21 Can I **learn** to be a **nurse** and **work** all around the **world**?
    Burt **stirred** the **fire** and **turned** the meat on the grill.

22 Farmer Brown takes **care** of her **large horse** every **morning**.
    Aren't you going to read the **warning** on the **chart**?

23 The **thoughtless** boy was cold **because** he **threw** away his jacket.
    It's **wonderful** to **watch water** flow over a cliff.

24 Take two **dollars** to the store and buy some **sugar**.
    Doctor Hunter said my leg will be **better** in **forty** days.

25 Her **nephew** was **unhappy** when he lost the **photograph**.
    Happily, his **cough** was better by **Friday**.

26 My **neighbor** thinks she saw a **ghost climb** on a tree **limb**.
    The postman **knew** the **wrong** name was **written** on the letter.

27 If you work too **quickly**, you will make **careless** mistakes.
    Everyone is **joyful** when Tina tells her **funniest** jokes.

28 I **heard Mother** call out a **friendly** greeting **early** this morning.
    Measure some milk and **break** an egg into the bowl.

29 **Our** mother **wrote** her letter on a **piece** of pretty paper.
    We must **wait** an **hour** for the bus that goes to **their** house.

30 It's **all right** to open the **beautiful presents** now.
    People went **straight** to the **hospital** after the train crash.

Building **Spelling** Skills

said

ask

stand

catch

eight

afraid

away

always

playing

waved

takes

than

great

they

prey

_____
bonus word

_____
bonus word

Building **Spelling** Skills

next

left

help

please

believe

many

very

been

seen

she

between

three

easy

sea

leave

_____
bonus word

_____
bonus word

Building **Spelling** Skills

pitch

drink

swim

life

while

I

my

light

buy

eye

which

find

why

kind

try

_____
bonus word

_____
bonus word

cut

cut

rocket

pocket

hold

told

often

grow

throne

so

sew

most

almost

both

coach

open

also

_____
bonus word

_____
bonus word

under

such

much

young

touch

use

your

you

unit

cute

few

new

fuel

human

music

_____
bonus word

_____
bonus word

cut

save

give

have

live

move

above

alive

alike

to

two

too

know

do

blew

blue

_____
bonus word

_____
bonus word

cut

missed	swimming	way
willing	swam	these
balloon	getting	niece
spelling	coming	might
pretty	came	show
still	having	float
off	doing	brain
added	ended	mean
letter	happened	close
different	happening	tried
pattern	started	cube
middle	joked	uniform
Mississippi	received	stayed
zipper	smiled	price
carry	smiling	usually

cut

cut

_____
bonus word

_____
bonus word

_____
bonus word

_____
bonus word

_____
bonus word

_____
bonus word

Building Spelling Skills
NAME
WEEK 10

Building Spelling Skills
NAME
WEEK 11

Building Spelling Skills
NAME
WEEK 12

Week 10	Week 11	Week 12
children	into	awful
search	today	called
teacher	without	falling
reached	something	mall
think	become	small
together	upon	straw
with	myself	drawing
where	everybody	strongest
everywhere	everyone	longer
short	maybe	song
push	outside	along
finish	basketball	bought
sure	homework	brought
who	skateboard	rough
whole	earthquake	tough

_____
bonus word

_____
bonus word

lady	looked	pointing
ladies	good	oily
surprise	brook	boy
surprises	football	voice
toys	cookie	oyster
shoes	stood	voyage
shy	full	loyal
cry	put	joined
cried	food	coin
study	school	choice
studied	truth	poison
story	room	destroy
only	true	enjoy
finally	chew	choose
family	due	chocolate

cut

cut

_____
bonus word

_____
bonus word

_____
bonus word

_____
bonus word

_____
bonus word

_____
bonus word

Building Spelling Skills

don't

didn't

I'll

I'm

it's

let's

you're

we're

doesn't

o'clock

won't

wouldn't

its

can't

that's

_____
bonus word

_____
bonus word

Building Spelling Skills

follow

below

own

grown

town

ground

around

found

about

house

group

would

should

country

cousin

_____
bonus word

_____
bonus word

Building Spelling Skills

April

babies

over

hello

even

we

silent

tiny

menu

future

dear

raise

white

used

those

_____
bonus word

_____
bonus word

cut

cut

disagree

again

given

other

money

problem

does

of

some

laid

change

tired

read

nice

lower

_____
bonus word

_____
bonus word

city

cereal

face

could

guess

huge

age

danger

goose

gone

coast

clean

guard

giant

carton

_____
bonus word

_____
bonus word

word

work

world

were

first

girl

turned

learn

bird

fire

here

nurse

jury

stirred

wear

_____
bonus word

_____
bonus word

cut

cut

aren't	threw	color
partner	through	odor
hard	thoughtless	farmer
chart	caught	calendar
farm	fault	dollar
start	taught	party
large	because	liar
more	one	after
before	once	number
horse	water	better
north	watch	doctor
morning	wanted	weather
care	wonder	every
stare	wonderful	forty
warning	walk	sugar

cut

cut

_____
bonus word

_____
bonus word

_____
bonus word

_____
bonus word

_____
bonus word

_____
bonus word

phone

photograph

orphan

alphabet

graph

nephew

enough

father

half

Friday

cough

unhappy

happier

happily

happiness

_____
bonus word

_____
bonus word

ghost

neighbor

high

knew

knot

unknown

rewrap

wrong

written

wrapper

unwrap

climb

limb

gnaw

gnat

_____
bonus word

_____
bonus word

useful

quietly

slowly

careful

careless

quickly

useless

worthless

fearful

fearless

joyful

smarter

fastest

funniest

happiest

_____
bonus word

_____
bonus word

cut

cut

brother

mother

another

field

friend

heard

early

friendly

head

near

year

shield

eat

measure

break

_____
bonus word

_____
bonus word

they're

there

their

soup

night

knight

right

write

weight

wait

piece

peace

hour

our

wrote

_____
bonus word

_____
bonus word

air

against

all right

until

presents

beautiful

favorite

clothes

people

vacation

remember

already

hospital

minute

straight

_____
bonus word

_____
bonus word

Spelling List

This Week's Focus:
- Spell short and long **a** words
- Spell words with the endings **-ed** and **-ing**
- Add the endings **-ed** and **-ing** after dropping the silent **e**
- Recognize the short **e** sound in **said**

STEP 1 Read and Spell

STEP 2 Copy and Spell

STEP 3 Cover and Spell

fold

1. said
2. ask
3. stand
4. catch
5. eight
6. afraid
7. away
8. always
9. playing
10. waved
11. takes
12. than
13. great
14. they
15. prey
16. _____ bonus word
17. _____ bonus word

Visual Memory

Fill in the boxes.

stand	waved	great	than	prey
afraid	they	playing	ask	takes
away	said	eight	catch	always

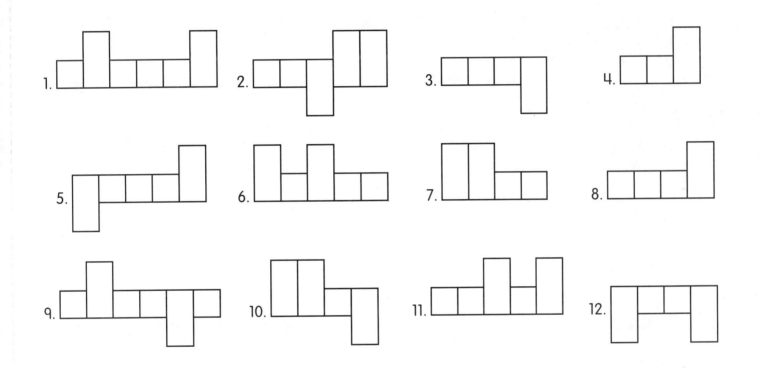

Cross out the misspelled words.

1. ~~sed~~   said

2. eitgh   eight

3. great   grait

4. prey   drey

5. catsh   catch

6. afraid   ufraid

7. wavd   waved

8. they   thay

9. aks   ask

10. stend   stand

11. playing   paling

12. taks   takes

13. than   fhan

14. away   uway

Word Meaning

Fill in the missing words.

takes	ask	always	catch	eight
afraid	away	stand	prey	waved
said	than	great	they	playing

1. An octopus uses its _____ arms to catch its _____.

2. It _____ a long time to _____ my dog to give him a bath.

3. My little sister is _____ _____ of thunder and lightning.

4. _____ were _____ football at the park.

5. Marcus _____ his hand and _____,"Good-bye."

6. You must _____ far _____ from the campfire.

My Spelling Dictation

Write the sentences. Circle the spelling words.

1. _____

_____

_____

2. _____

_____

_____

Word Study

Underline the words with the long **a** sound.
Circle the letters that make that sound.

w(a)ved   catch   away   takes   great

ask   eight   stand   said   they

always   afraid   prey   than   playing

An ending is a word part added at the end of a word.
Add **ed** and **ing** to each word.

	ed	ing
1. play	played	playing
2. ask	_____	_____
3. prey	_____	_____
4. paint	_____	_____

Drop the **e** and add the endings **ed** and **ing**.

1. wave	waved	waving
2. smile	_____	_____
3. skate	_____	_____
4. bake	_____	_____

Building Spelling Skills

Spelling List

This Week's Focus:
- Spell short **e** words
- Spell words with the long **e** sound spelled **ea**, **ie**, **ee**, **e**, and **y**
- Recognize the short **i** sound in **been**

STEP 1 Read and Spell	STEP 2 Copy and Spell	STEP 3 Cover and Spell
1. next		
2. left		
3. help		
4. please		
5. believe		
6. many		
7. very		
8. been		
9. seen		
10. she		
11. between		
12. three		
13. easy		
14. sea		
15. leave		
16. _____ bonus word		
17. _____ bonus word		

fold

Visual Memory

Fill in the boxes.

very	believe	next	easy	leave
been	please	help	between	she
seen	many	left	three	sea

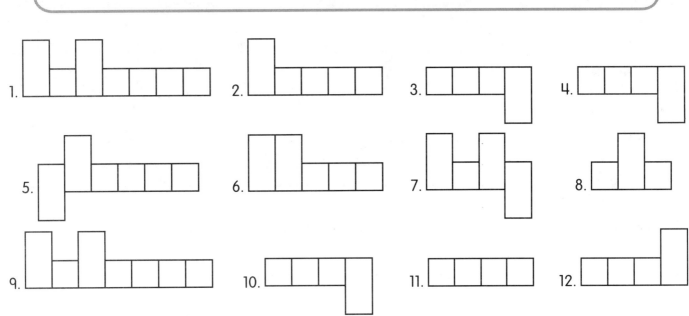

1.   2.   3.   4.

5.   6.   7.   8.

9.   10.   11.   12.

Circle the misspelled words. Write them correctly on the lines.

1. Plez help me fix my bike.   _____

2. We have to leaf now.   _____

3. It isn't eezy to ride a horse.   _____

4. Have you ben to the park?   _____

5. Park the car betwene the trees.   _____

6. Did you belive his story?   _____

7. I saw miny cows at his farm.   _____

8. Jane had tree pet cats.   _____

Word Meaning

Answer the questions.

next	left	help	please	believe
many	very	been	seen	she
between	three	easy	sea	leave

1. What comes after **two**? _____

2. What is another word for **ocean**? _____

3. What is the opposite of... ?

   difficult _____   stay _____

   right _____   harm _____

   few _____

4. Which word means "in the middle of two things"? _____

5. What word do you use if you want to show good manners? _____

6. Which word means you think something is true? _____

My Spelling Dictation

Write the sentences. Circle the spelling words.

1. _____

   _____

   _____

2. _____

   _____

   _____

Word Study

Underline the words with the long e sound.
Circle the letters that make that sound.

three   left   she

please   believe   many

very   been   seen

help   between   leave

easy   sea   next

Write the spelling words that rhyme with these words.

1. merry   _____

2. any   _____

3. sneeze   _____

4. free   _____

5. yelp   _____

6. pea   _____

7. queen   _____

8. relieve   _____

9. bee   _____

10. lean   _____

next	left	help	please	believe
many	very	been	seen	she
leave	three	easy	sea	between

Spelling List

This Week's Focus:
- Spell short and long **i** words
- Spell words in the **-ind**, **-ile**, **-ight**, and **-ink** word families

STEP 1 Read and Spell	STEP 2 Copy and Spell	STEP 3 Cover and Spell

fold

1. pitch
2. drink
3. swim
4. life
5. while
6. I
7. my
8. light
9. buy
10. eye
11. which
12. find
13. why
14. kind
15. try
16. _____ bonus word
17. _____ bonus word

Visual Memory

Fill in the boxes.

life	pitch	my	eye	why
drink	while	light	which	kind
try	I	buy	find	swim

1.
2.
3.
4.
5.
6.
7.
8.
9.
10.
11.
12.

Circle the misspelled words.
Write them correctly on the lines.

1. Mom needs to bie a lite for the lamp. _____ _____

2. Witch kind of drenk do you like best? _____ _____

3. Trie to catch the ball when I picth it. _____ _____

4. I get water in my aye when I swem. _____ _____

5. Eye like to by that kind of pen. _____ _____

Word Meaning

Fill in the missing words.

1. _____ have something in my _____.
   (I, try)   (why, eye)

2. _____ did you _____ that kind of soft _____?
   (Why, Try)   (buy, which)   (drink, pitch)

3. _____ kind of _____ do you need?
   (Which, Witch)   (while, light)

4. Can you catch _____ I _____ the baseball?
                   (while, light)   (why, pitch)

5. The words _____ and _____ rhyme.
              (my, find)   (try, while)

6. I have tried to be a _____ person all of my _____.
                        (find, kind)   (while, life)

My Spelling Dictation

Write the sentences. Circle the spelling words.

1. _____

   _____

   _____

2. _____

   _____

   _____

Word Study

Underline the words with the long **i** sound.
Circle the letters that make that sound.

life	drink	try
pitch	while	I
my	light	buy
eye	which	find
why	kind	swim

Add letters to make new words.
Then read all the words in each word family.

ind	ile	ight	ink
_____find	_____ile	_____ight	_____ink
_____ind	_____ile	_____ight	_____ink
_____ind	_____ile	_____ight	_____ink
_____ind	_____ile	_____ight	_____ink

Spelling List

This Week's Focus:
- Spell words with the long **o** sound
- Distinguish between one- and two-syllable words

STEP 1 Read and Spell

1. rocket
2. pocket
3. hold
4. told
5. often
6. grow
7. throne
8. so
9. sew
10. most
11. almost
12. both
13. coach
14. open
15. also
16. _____
    bonus word
17. _____
    bonus word

STEP 2 Copy and Spell

STEP 3 Cover and Spell

fold

Fill in the boxes.

rocket	hold	often	grow	so
pocket	told	also	sew	most
throne	almost	both	coach	open

1.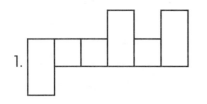

2.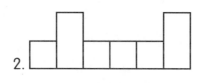

3.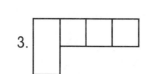

4.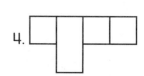

5.

6.

7.

8.

9.

10.

11.

12.

Cross out the misspelled words.

1. roket   rocket

2. whold   hold

3. often   offen

4. throne   thone

5. amolst   almost

6. both   bofh

7. coach   koach

8. allso   also

9. opun   open

10. grow   groe

11. told   tole

12. sowe   sew

Word Meaning

Answer the questions.

rocket	hold	often	grow	so
pocket	most	also	sew	told
throne	almost	both	coach	open

1. What could a king or queen sit on? _____

2. In what part of a jacket can you carry things? _____

3. Which two spelling words rhyme with **cold**?

   _____ _____

4. Which two spelling words sound the same
   but have different spellings?

   _____ _____

5. What is the opposite of **shut**? _____

6. What transportation would an astronaut use? _____

My Spelling Dictation

Write the sentences. Circle the spelling words.

1. _____

   _____

   _____

2. _____

   _____

Word Study

Underline the words with the long **o** sound.
Circle the letters that make that sound.

g r o w	h o l d	t h r o n e
r o c k e t	s o	p o c k e t
t o l d	a l s o	s e w
m o s t	o f t e n	a l m o s t
b o t h	c o a c h	o p e n

Say each word.

rocket	hold	often	both	almost
grow	so	pocket	coach	throne
told	also	sew	open	most

Write the words with one syllable.

1. _____
2. _____
3. _____
4. _____
5. _____
6. _____
7. _____
8. _____
9. _____

Write the words with two syllables.

1. _____
2. _____
3. _____
4. _____
5. _____
6. _____

Spelling List

This Week's Focus:
- Spell words with the short and long **u** sounds
- Spell words with an initial /**y**/ sound

STEP 1 Read and Spell	STEP 2 Copy and Spell	STEP 3 Cover and Spell
1. under		
2. such		
3. much		
4. young		
5. touch		
6. use		
7. your		
8. you		
9. unit		
10. cute		
11. few		
12. new		
13. fuel		
14. human		
15. music		
16. _____ bonus word		
17. _____ bonus word		

fold

Visual Memory

Unscramble the letters to make spelling words.

under	such	much	young	touch
use	your	you	unit	fuel
few	new	cute	human	music

1. chum _____

2. outch _____

3. sue _____

4. uoy _____

5. intu _____

6. wef _____

7. lufe _____

8. redun _____

9. chus _____

10. hunam _____

11. sicmu _____

12. gnuoy _____

Circle the misspelled words. Write them correctly on the lines.

1. Jim's dog ran undar the bed. _____

2. Do you like her noo coat? _____

3. What is yer name? _____

4. That's a kute baby. _____

5. Don't tuch the hot stove! _____

6. Ann's sister is a yung lady. _____

7. A fuo boys came to the party. _____

8. Do you like rap moosic? _____

 Building Spelling Skills, Daily Practice • EMC 2707

Word Meaning

Draw a picture to show what each sentence means.

Kate found her kitten hiding under the bed.	Dad pumped fuel into the tank of his new car.
The young boy played music.	A few pennies were in the cute piggy bank.

My Spelling Dictation

Write the sentences. Circle the spelling words.

1. _____

_____

_____

2. _____

_____

Word Study

Underline the words with the long **u** sound.
Circle the letters that make that sound.

u s e	s u c h	f e w
y o u n g	m u s i c	u n d e r
y o u r	y o u	u n i t
c u t e	m u c h	n e w
f u e l	h u m a n	t o u c h

Write the spelling words that rhyme with these words.

1. crutch   _____   6. flute   _____

2. sung   _____   7. few   _____

3. thunder   _____   8. jewel   _____

4. shoes   _____   9. Dutch   _____

5. too   _____   10. tour   _____

Fill in the blanks with rhyming word pairs from above.

1. Zeke hid _____ the bed when he heard _____.

2. They bought a _____ pairs of _____ shoes.

3. A _____ little girl played music on her _____.

WEEK 6

Spelling List

This Week's Focus:
- Spell words that end with a silent **e**
- Spell homophones
- Compare past and present tense verbs

STEP 1 Read and Spell	STEP 2 Copy and Spell	STEP 3 Cover and Spell

fold

1. save

2. give

3. have

4. live

5. move

6. above

7. alive

8. alike

9. to

10. two

11. too

12. know

13. do

14. blew

15. blue

16. _____
bonus word

17. _____
bonus word

Visual Memory

Fill in the missing letters.

save	give	have	live	move
above	alike	alive	to	two
too	know	do	blew	blue

_____oo   _____ike   _____ew   _____ow

_____ue   _____wo   _____o   _____o

_____ove   _____ove   _____ave   _____ave

_____ive   _____ive   _____ive

Circle the misspelled words.
Write them correctly on the lines.

1. There were tow plants in the pot.   _____

2. The girls looked ulike.   _____

3. His new bike is blew.   _____

4. Do you no what fish like to eat?   _____

5. May I hav a ride to school?   _____

6. Will you geve me some milk?   _____

7. Nat went too the zoo.   _____

8. Moov your bike out of the street.   _____

Word Meaning

Homophones are words that sound alike but have different spellings and meanings.

Choose the correct homophone for each sentence.

1. That little boy is _____ years old.
   (to, two, too)

2. I want an ice-cream cone, _____.
   (to, two, too)

3. Bring the plates _____ the table.
   (to, two, too)

4. A strong wind _____ the leaves off the trees.
   (blew, blue)

5. Did you see how _____ the sky was today?
   (blew, blue)

6. When will you _____ if you can go on the trip?
   (know, no)

7. There is _____ more peanut butter in the jar.
   (know, no)

My Spelling Dictation

Write the sentences. Circle the spelling words.

1. _____

   _____

   _____

2. _____

   _____

Word Study

A present tense verb tells about what is happening **NOW**.
A past tense verb tells about what happened before.
Use the spelling list to find the present tense for each past tense verb.
Write the present tense words on the lines.

past tense	present tense	past tense	present tense
1. gave	_____	5. blew	_____
2. moved	_____	6. did	_____
3. lived	_____	7. had	_____
4. knew	_____	8. saved	_____

Fill in the correct verb form.

1. New people just _____ in next door.
   (move)

2. Do you _____ how to make toast?
   (know)

3. The man _____ up balloons and made animals out of them.
   (blow)

4. Have you _____ the money you need for a new bike?
   (save)

Draw lines to match these words to their opposites.

alive   different

alike   below

above   dead

Spelling List

This Week's Focus:
- Spell words with double consonants
- Divide words into syllables

STEP 1 Read and Spell	STEP 2 Copy and Spell	STEP 3 Cover and Spell
1. missed		
2. willing		
3. balloon		
4. spelling		
5. pretty		
6. still		
7. off		
8. added		
9. letter		
10. different		
11. pattern		
12. middle		
13. Mississippi		
14. zipper		
15. carry		
16. _____ bonus word		
17. _____ bonus word		

fold

Find the words hiding in this puzzle.

```
m  b  a  l  l  o  o  n  o  f  f  x  l
i  i  l  l  z  i  p  m  i  d  d  l  e
s  o  s  w  i  l  l  i  n  g  i  z  t
s  c  a  s  s  y  z  g  o  o  f  a  t
e  t  s  t  i  l  l  i  u  v  f  d  e
d  g  i  p  a  s  l  i  p  p  e  d  r
c  o  l  r  o  w  s  n  o  p  r  e  p
a  z  l  e  t  t  r  i  n  e  e  d  r
r  p  a  t  t  e  r  n  p  l  n  r  e
r  o  p  t  d  i  f  f  u  p  t  z  t
y  f  e  y  o  s  p  e  l  l  i  n  g
```

added
balloon
carry
different
letter
middle
missed
Mississippi
off
pattern
pretty
spelling
still
willing
zipper

Circle the correct spelling.

1. misst	missed	mised	missd
2. baloon	balon	ballon	balloon
3. pretty	pertty	preddy	prety
4. ledder	eter	leter	letter
5. differunt	different	diferent	diffrent
6. patturn	patern	pattern	pattren
7. carry	cerry	karry	kerry
8. ziper	zippir	zipper	zippre

Fill in the missing words.

added	balloon	carry	different	pattern
middle	missed	off	Mississippi	letter
pretty	spelling	still	willing	zipper

1. Did you study for the _____ test?

2. We sailed on the _____ River.

3. I bought a shiny red _____ for my little sister.

4. The _____ on her jacket broke.

5. Will you help me _____ this box into the house?

6. Who wrote you that _____?

7. I went to a _____ school last year.

8. Mother cut out the _____ for a new dress she is making.

My Spelling Dictation

Write the sentences. Circle the spelling words.

1. _____

   _____

   _____

2. _____

   _____

   _____

Word Study

Divide these words into syllables.
Remember the rules:

- If a word has double consonants in the middle, divide between them.
- If a word has an ending, divide between the base word and the ending.

1. balloon _____bal loon_____

2. spelling _____spell ing_____

3. pretty _____

4. letter _____

5. added _____

6. pattern _____

7. zipper _____

8. willing _____

9. middle _____

10. carry _____

11. missing _____

12. Mississippi _____

Fill in the missing double consonants to make spelling words.

1. spe_____ing

2. o_____

3. sti_____

4. mi_____le

5. pa_____ern

6. mi_____ed

7. di_____erent

8. Mi_____i_____i_____i

Spelling List

This Week's Focus:
- Spell verbs that end with **-ing** or **-ed**
- Spell irregular past tense verbs

STEP 1 Read and Spell	STEP 2 Copy and Spell	STEP 3 Cover and Spell

fold

1. swimming

2. swam

3. getting

4. coming

5. came

6. having

7. doing

8. ended

9. happened

10. happening

11. started

12. joked

13. received

14. smiled

15. smiling

16. _____
   bonus word

17. _____
   bonus word

Visual Memory

Circle the missing letters. Fill in the blanks.

1. swi___mm___ing	m	(mm)	
2. ca_____e	m	mm	
3. ge_____ing	t	tt	
4. star_____ed	t	tt	
5. en_____ed	d	dd	
6. ha_____ened	p	pp	

7. smi_____ed	l	ll	
8. sti_____	l	ll	
9. swa_____	m	mm	
10. co_____ing	m	mm	
11. jo_____ed	k	kk	
12. recei_____ed	v	vv	

Write the correct spelling of these words.

1. swiming _____

2. geting _____

3. comeng _____

4. haveng _____

5. dooing _____

6. happend _____

7. happining _____

8. joket _____

9. smild _____

10. kame _____

Fill in the missing word. Use the correct ending.

1. Raul _____ piano lessons last week.
   (start)

2. Have you _____ your birthday present yet?
   (receive)

3. Why is she _____?
   (smile)

Word Meaning

Fill in the correct form of the missing words.

1. We _____ in the river yesterday.
   (swam, swimming)

2. They are going _____ today.
   (swam, swimming)

3. What is _____ on that television program?
   (happened, happening)

4. That is the same thing that _____ on the last show.
   (happened, happening)

5. Who is _____ to the band concert?
   (came, coming)

6. Many people _____ to hear us play last year.
   (came, coming)

7. Karen _____ when she opened the front door.
   (smiling, smiled)

8. Why was she _____?
   (smiling, smiled)

My Spelling Dictation

Write the sentences. Circle the spelling words.

1. _____

_____

_____

2. _____

_____

_____

Word Study

Write the past tense of these words.
Use the spelling list.

1. joke _____

2. swim _____

3. happen _____

4. come _____

5. end _____

6. smile _____

7. receive _____

8. start _____

Add the ending **ing** to each base word.
What did you do to spell the word correctly?

	no change	double final consonant	drop **e**
1. swim**ming**		✔	
2. get_____			
3. receive_____			
4. come_____			
5. have_____			
6. do_____			
7. smile_____			
8. end_____			
9. happen_____			
10. start_____			
11. joke_____			

Spelling List

This Week's Focus:
- Spell words with long vowel sounds
- Add **-ed** to verbs

STEP 1 Read and Spell

fold

1. way
2. these
3. niece
4. might
5. show
6. float
7. brain
8. mean
9. close
10. tried
11. cube
12. uniform
13. stayed
14. price
15. usually
16. _____
   bonus word
17. _____
   bonus word

STEP 2 Copy and Spell

STEP 3 Cover and Spell

Unscramble the words. Match them to the correct spelling.

1. yaw	close	8. beuc	price
2. thees	niece	9. ripce	float
3. neice	way	10. mitgh	cube
4. hows	these	11. foalt	uniform
5. anme	tried	12. niarb	brain
6. locse	mean	13. formuni	stayed
7. deirt	show	14. edstay	might

Circle the misspelled words.
Write them correctly on the lines.

1. My new band youniform is silver. _____

2. Cloze the door when you go out. _____

3. The boys mite go fishing next Saturday. _____

4. Put an ice kube in that glass. _____

5. Grandpa staid in bed until 8 o'clock. _____

6. The fox tryed to catch a rabbit. _____

7. Can you shoo me how to play this game? _____

8. Did you ever drink a root beer flote? _____

Word Meaning

Complete the crossword puzzle.

Across

1. not kind
4. the cost
5. special clothing
8. to shut
9. this one and this one

Down

2. a girl relative
3. what you think with
6. the opposite of **sink**
7. a six-sided square
10. to remain

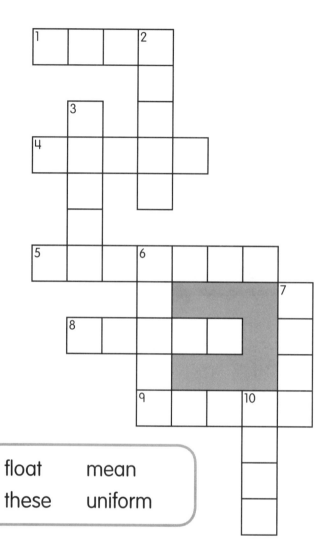

brain	close	cube	float	mean
niece	price	stay	these	uniform

My Spelling Dictation

Write the sentences. Circle the spelling words.

1. _____

_____

_____

2. _____

_____

_____

Word Study

Circle the letters that make the long vowel sound.
Write the long vowel sound you hear on the line.

1. w(a y) __a__

2. these ____

3. niece ____

4. show ____

5. float ____

6. brain ____

7. mean ____

8. close ____

9. tried ____

10. cube ____

11. uniform ____

12. stayed ____

13. price ____

Add **ed** to the words. Write the words in the correct column.

	no change	change **y** to **i**
1. stay	stayed	____
2. try	____	____
3. float	____	____
4. show	____	____
5. cry	____	____
6. hurry	____	____
7. plant	____	____
8. worry	____	____
9. play	____	____
10. scurry	____	____

WEEK 10

Spelling List

This Week's Focus:
- Spell words with consonant digraphs **ch**, **sh**, **th**, and **wh**
- Identify the number of syllables in a word
- Recognize the /sh/ sound in **sure**

STEP 1 Read and Spell

STEP 2 Copy and Spell

STEP 3 Cover and Spell

fold

1. children
2. search
3. teacher
4. reached
5. think
6. together
7. with
8. where
9. everywhere
10. short
11. push
12. finish
13. sure
14. who
15. whole
16. _____
   bonus word
17. _____
   bonus word

Circle all the words that are spelled correctly.

reacht	finush	search
teatcher	whol	where
children	with	chilren
whith	shure	who
think	push	serch
everywere	sure	teacher
whole	poosh	thinck

Circle the misspelled words.
Write them correctly on the lines.

1. Hoo ate that hole cake?

   _____   _____

2. Can the childrun poosh the wagon?

   _____   _____

3. We can go when you finnish the shurt story.

   _____   _____

4. Where do you tink we should serch for it?

   _____   _____

5. Will you and your teecher go there togepher?

   _____   _____

Word Meaning

Answer the questions.

children	search	teacher	reached	think
together	with	where	short	push
everywhere	finish	sure	who	whole

1. Which ones are names for people?

   _____   _____

2. Which word means "all places"?   _____

3. What do you do when you use your brain?   _____

4. Which word means "to complete something"?   _____

5. Which word means "to look for something
   that is lost"?   _____

6. What is the opposite of...?

   part _____   long _____   apart _____

My Spelling Dictation

Write the sentences. Circle the spelling words.

1. _____

   _____

   _____

2. _____

   _____

   _____

Word Study

Fill in the missing letters to make spelling words.
Write **ch**, **th**, **wh**, or **sh**.

1. __ch__ildren

2. sear____

3. ____ink

4. ____ole

5. ____ere

6. fini____

7. toge____er

8. pu____

9. tea____er

10. wi____

11. ____ort

12. ____o

Read the words.
Circle the number of syllables you hear.

1. together   1 2 3 4

2. who   1 2 3 4

3. search   1 2 3 4

4. teacher   1 2 3 4

5. reached   1 2 3 4

6. think   1 2 3 4

7. with   1 2 3 4

8. everywhere   1 2 3 4

9. sure   1 2 3 4

10. children   1 2 3 4

11. whole   1 2 3 4

12. finish   1 2 3 4

13. push   1 2 3 4

14. where   1 2 3 4

15. short   1 2 3 4

Spelling List

This Week's Focus:
- Spell compound words
- Divide compound words into syllables

STEP 1 Read and Spell	**STEP 2** Copy and Spell	**STEP 3** Cover and Spell

fold

1. into
2. today
3. without
4. something
5. become
6. upon
7. myself
8. everybody
9. everyone
10. maybe
11. outside
12. basketball
13. homework
14. skateboard
15. earthquake
16. _____
   bonus word
17. _____
   bonus word

Visual Memory

Find the words hiding in this puzzle.

```
e  v  e  r  y  b  o  d  y  e  s  s
v  a  n  h  o  m  e  w  o  r  k  o
e  r  r  t  o  d  a  y  m  a  a  m
r  w  i  t  h  o  u  t  y  b  t  e
y  o  u  i  h  e  r  o  s  e  e  t
o  u  t  n  o  q  u  d  e  c  b  h
n  e  w  t  t  u  u  y  l  o  o  i
e  u  p  o  n  t  o  a  f  m  a  n
m  a  y  b  e  m  y  s  k  e  r  g
o  u  t  o  u  t  s  i  d  e  d  o
b  a  s  k  e  t  b  a  l  l  i  n
```

become
basketball
earthquake
everybody
everyone
homework
into
maybe
myself
outside
skateboard
something
today
upon
without

Circle the 10 misspelled words.
Write them correctly on the lines.

   Yesterday I finished my homewerk by misef. Then I went owtside
and rode my skatbord to the park. Everbody was playing baskutball.

   Evrywon was having fun when sumthing happened. The ground
started to shake. It was an erthquak! When it stopped, we ran home
wifout the basketball. Maybe it is still at the park.

_____   _____

_____   _____

_____   _____

_____   _____

Word Meaning

Fill in the missing words.

become	basketball	upon	into	everyone
homework	skateboard	maybe	myself	outside
something	earthquake	today	without	everybody

1. Maurice received a _____ for his birthday.

2. An _____ made cracks in the walls of our house.

3. Our teacher said, "There is no _____ _____!"

4. _____ strange ran _____ the barn.

5. Once _____ a time, there was a dragon that couldn't fly.

6. Do you want to _____ a professional soccer player someday?

7. Can you wash the car _____ any help?

8. _____ is gone, so I am all by _____.

My Spelling Dictation

Write the sentences. Circle the spelling words.

1. _____

_____

_____

2. _____

_____

Word Study

Use the words in the word box to make compound words.

with	up	to	thing	quake
board	ball	day	every	body
come	side	my	may	home

1. basket ball _____

2. be _____

3. earth _____

4. every _____

5. _____ one

6. _____ work

7. in _____

8. _____ self

9. _____ be

10. out _____

11. skate _____

12. some _____

13. to _____

14. _____ on

15. _____ out

Divide these words into syllables.

1. in|to

2. today

3. without

4. become

5. something

6. maybe

7. outside

8. homework

9. earthquake

Did you discover a new rule here about dividing words into syllables?   Yes   No

What is it? _____

Spelling List

This Week's Focus:
- Spell words with the vowel sound in **small**, **straw**, **song**, and **bought**
- Spell words with the short **u** sound spelled **ough**
- Add the endings -**er** and -**est**

STEP 1 Read and Spell

STEP 2 Copy and Spell

STEP 3 Cover and Spell

fold

1. awful
2. called
3. falling
4. mall
5. small
6. straw
7. drawing
8. strongest
9. longer
10. song
11. along
12. bought
13. brought
14. rough
15. tough
16. _____
   bonus word
17. _____
   bonus word

Visual Memory

Unscramble the words. Write them on the lines.

falling	awful	called	mall	straw
small	drawing	strongest	longer	tough
song	along	bought	brought	rough

1. awflu _____

2. decall _____

3. llam _____

4. gons _____

5. malls _____

6. olang _____

7. rouhg _____

8. lnoger _____

9. traws _____

10. darwing _____

11. srongtest _____

12. flaling _____

Circle the misspelled words. Write them correctly on the lines.

1. Adam made an ahful mistake.

   _____

2. Put the smal starw in the cold drink.

   _____ _____

3. He made a drawn of the stronust man in the world.

   _____ _____

4. Anna bawght it at the moll.

   _____ _____

5. Will you sing a longar sogn next time?

   _____ _____

Word Meaning

Answer the questions.

falling	awful	called	mall	straw
small	drawing	strongest	longer	tough
song	along	bought	brought	rough

1. Which word means "terrible"? _____

2. What could be used to make a bed for a farm animal? _____

3. What do you call a place with many shops all together? _____

4. Which word is a kind of picture? _____

5. What is the opposite of...?

   sold _____   shorter _____

   large _____   weakest _____

6. What does **straw** mean in this sentence? Circle your answer.
   I used a plastic straw to drink my milk.

   a. dried hay   b. thin, hollow tube   c. material for making popcorn

My Spelling Dictation

Write the sentences. Circle the spelling words.

1. _____

_____

_____

2. _____

_____

_____

Word Study

Underline the words with the sound of **a** in **all**.
Circle the letters that make the sound.

(aw)ful	called	tough
mall	song	along
rough	bought	straw
strongest	falling	brought
small	drawing	longer

Add **er** or **est** to make a comparison.

	er	est
1. strong	_____	_____
2. long	_____	_____
3. small	_____	_____
4. rough	_____	_____
5. tough	_____	_____

6. That wrestler is the _____ man I've ever seen.
   (strong)

7. Is a rabbit _____ than a cat?
   (small)

8. Mrs. Martin has the _____ bath towels I've ever felt.
   (rough)

9. Billy thinks he is the _____ kid on our block.
   (tough)

10. The yellow bus is _____ than our truck.
    (long)

Spelling List

This Week's Focus:
- Spell words with the long **e** and long **i** sounds spelled **y**
- Spell the plural forms of words by adding **s**, **es**, or **ies**
- Spell the past tense of words by changing **y** to **i** and adding **ed**

STEP 1 Read and Spell	STEP 2 Copy and Spell	STEP 3 Cover and Spell

fold

1. lady
2. ladies
3. surprise
4. surprises
5. toys
6. shoes
7. shy
8. cry
9. cried
10. study
11. studied
12. story
13. only
14. finally
15. family
16. _____ *bonus word*
17. _____ *bonus word*

Fill in the missing syllable to make spelling words.

1. la_dy_____

2. _____ily

3. on_____

4. _____prises

5. _____dies

6. stud_____

7. fi_____ly

8. _____y

9. _____ied

10. sur_____

Circle the misspelled words.
Write them correctly on the lines.

1. The children gave Mother a big suprise.   _____

2. Put on your shoos before you go outside.   _____

3. The baby cryed for his bottle.   _____

4. Do you have a big famuly?   _____

5. Two ladys sang a song.   _____

6. Did you enjoy the storie?   _____

7. The game was finelly over.   _____

8. Have you studied for the math test?   _____

Word Meaning

Fill in the missing words.

1. What _____ was in that large box?
   (surprise, surprises)

2. Both _____ bought new hats.
   (lady, ladies)

3. Did he _____ clean his bedroom?
   (finally, family)

4. She wants to _____ the violin.
   (study, studied)

5. My grandfather is full of funny _____ that make me laugh.
   (surprise, surprises)

6. I _____ for a long time when my best friend moved away.
   (cry, cried)

My Spelling Dictation

Write the sentences. Circle the spelling words.

1. _____

   _____

   _____

2. _____

   _____

   _____

Word Study

Write the words in the correct boxes.

| cry | only | story | my | study | fly |
| lady | why | family | funny | shy | try |

y says **i**	**y** says **e**
cry	

Write the plural forms. Mark how you changed each word.

	add **s**	drop **e**, add **es**	change **y** to **i** and add **es**
1. lady _ladies_			✔
2. toy _____			
3. story _____			
4. shoe _____			
5. family _____			
6. rocket _____			
7. niece _____			

Spelling List

This Week's Focus:
- Spell words with the vowel sounds in **push** and **do**

STEP 1 Read and Spell	STEP 2 Copy and Spell	STEP 3 Cover and Spell

1. looked
2. good
3. brook
4. football
5. cookie
6. stood
7. full
8. put
9. food
10. school
11. truth
12. room
13. true
14. chew
15. due
16. _____ bonus word
17. _____ bonus word

Visual Memory

Find the words hiding in the puzzle.

```
f  g  t  r  u  t  h  c  h  f
l  o  o  k  e  d  r  o  c  u
f  o  o  d  o  o  k  o  o  l
t  d  p  t  c  h  e  w  o  l
r  u  u  u  b  r  o  o  k  m
u  e  s  p  t  a  t  h  i  h
e  s  c  h  o  o  l  x  e  e
n  o  s  t  o  o  d  l  m  w
```

brook	looked
chew	put
cookie	room
due	school
food	stood
football	true
full	truth
good	

Circle the misspelled words.
Write them correctly on the lines.

1. luked

2. good

3. brook

4. futbal

5. cookee

6. fud

7. full

8. poot

9. stood

10. schol

11. truth

12. doo

13. chu

14. true

15. ruum

_____ _____ _____

_____ _____ _____

_____ _____ _____

73

Word Meaning

Complete the crossword puzzle.

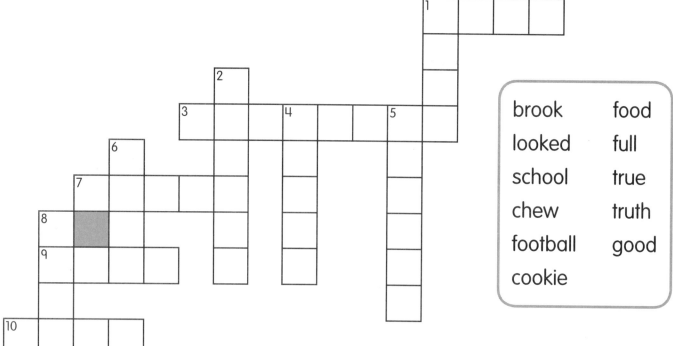

brook food

looked full

school true

chew truth

football good

cookie

Across

1. something to eat
3. a type of sports equipment
7. a small stream
9. to crush with your teeth
10. the opposite of **bad**

Down

1. the opposite of **empty**
2. a sweet treat
4. always tell the ____
5. used your eyes to see
6. not a lie
8. where you go to learn

My Spelling Dictation

Write the sentences. Circle the spelling words.

1. _____

_____

_____

2. _____

_____

Word Study

Write the words in the correct boxes.

looked	good	truth	put	stood
food	brook	room	true	full
football	school	cookie	chew	due

sound of **u** in **push**	sound of **o** in **do**
looked	

Use the spelling list to find words that are the opposite.

1. empty _____

2. awful _____

3. sat _____

4. remove _____

5. lie _____

6. false _____

© Evan-Moor Corp.

75

Building Spelling Skills, Daily Practice • EMC 2707

Spelling List

This Week's Focus:
- Spell words with **oy** and **oi**
- Spell words with the initial digraph **ch**
- Add the endings -**s**, -**es**, -**ed**, and -**ing**

STEP 1 Read and Spell	STEP 2 Copy and Spell	STEP 3 Cover and Spell

fold

1. pointing

2. oily

3. boy

4. voice

5. oyster

6. voyage

7. loyal

8. joined

9. coin

10. choice

11. poison

12. destroy

13. enjoy

14. choose

15. chocolate

16. _____
     bonus word

17. _____
     bonus word

Unscramble the words. Match them to the correct spelling.

1. yoil   voice

2. cevoi   oily

3. soyter   boy

4. joyen   voyage

5. yob   oyster

6. agevoy   loyal

7. loyla   enjoy

8. ocin   coin

9. ingpoint   joined

10. cocholate   choice

11. edjoin   chocolate

12. oichce   pointing

13. sonpoi   destroy

14. troydes   poison

Circle the misspelled words. Write them correctly on the lines.

1. My choyse is chocklate.

_____   _____

2. Did you injoy your voyege?

_____   _____

3. He will distroy the weeds without using poisen.

_____   _____

4. The little doy is pointing at an oister.

_____   _____

5. Which coyn did he chose?

_____   _____

Fill in the missing words.

1. We ate _____ on our sea _____.
   (coins, oysters)   (poison, voyage)

2. _____ cake is always Paul's _____.
   (Oyster, Chocolate)   (choose, choice)

3. Did that _____ _____ his toy truck?
   (joined, boy)   (destroy, loyal)

4. Why are you _____ at that gold _____?
   (pointing, oily)   (joined, coin)

5. Don't use a loud _____ while the baby is taking a nap.
   (choice, voice)

6. Lock the box of insect _____ in a cupboard.
   (chocolate, poison)

My Spelling Dictation

Write the sentences. Circle the spelling words.

1. _____

   _____

   _____

2. _____

   _____

   _____

Word Study

Fill in the missing sounds. Write **oi** or **oy**.

1. b_____   4. _____ster   7. p_____son   10. c_____n

2. _____ly   5. v_____ce   8. p_____nting   11. enj_____

3. ch_____ce   6. l_____al   9. destr_____   12. j_____ned

Add endings to change the verbs.

s or es	ed	ing
1. point _____points_____	_____	_____
2. join _____	_____	_____
3. smile _____	_____	_____
4. finish _____	_____	_____

Add the correct endings to the verbs.

1. Norman was _____ at the funny television show.
   (smile)

2. The short hand on a clock always _____ to the hour.
   (point)

3. Betty always _____ her work before she plays.
   (finish)

4. Carlos is _____ the Boy Scouts.
   (join)

Spelling List

This Week's Focus:
- Spell contractions
- Recognize homophones **it's** and **its**

STEP 1 Read and Spell

STEP 2 Copy and Spell

STEP 3 Cover and Spell

fold

1. don't
2. didn't
3. I'll
4. I'm
5. it's
6. let's
7. you're
8. we're
9. doesn't
10. o'clock
11. won't
12. wouldn't
13. its
14. can't
15. that's
16. _____ bonus word
17. _____ bonus word

Visual Memory

A contraction is a word formed from two words by leaving out some letters. An apostrophe is used to replace the letters.

Write the apostrophe in the correct place in these contractions.

1. don't
2. didnt
3. Ill
4. thats
5. its

6. cant
7. lets
8. youre
9. were
10. doesnt

11. oclock
12. wont
13. Im
14. wouldnt

Circle the misspelled words.
Write them correctly on the lines.

1. They din't like the scary movie. _____

2. Did you know were moving when school is out? _____

3. Why duzn't the clock work? _____

4. Your going to Disneyland next week! _____

5. Tat's Cindy's pet hamster. _____

6. Its too hot to play outside today. _____

7. Let's ask why they kan't come over. _____

8. A'll bring my football to the game. _____

Word Meaning

Write the contractions to complete the crossword puzzle.
Don't forget to include the apostrophe.

Down

1. cannot
2. I will
3. does not
5. do not
6. of the clock
7. it is
8. we are

Across

4. would not
8. will not
9. that is
10. you are
11. let us

My Spelling Dictation

Write the sentences. Circle the spelling words.

1. _____

_____

_____

2. _____

_____

_____

Word Study

Answer the questions.

1. What is the long form of these words?

   won't _____   don't _____

2. Which spelling means "belonging to it"?   its   it's

3. Which spelling means "I will"?   Ill   I'll

What letter or letters are removed to make the contraction?

	contractions	missing letters
1. do not	don't	o
2. we are	_____	_____
3. they are	_____	_____
4. it is	_____	_____
5. would not	_____	_____
6. cannot	_____	_____
7. I am	_____	_____
8. that is	_____	_____
9. does not	_____	_____
10. did not	_____	_____
11. I will	_____	_____
12. let us	_____	_____

Spelling List

This Week's Focus:
- Spell words with the vowel digraphs **ow** and **ou**

STEP 1 Read and Spell

STEP 2 Copy and Spell

STEP 3 Cover and Spell

1. follow
2. below
3. own
4. grown
5. town
6. ground
7. around
8. found
9. about
10. house
11. group
12. would
13. should
14. country
15. cousin
16. _____ bonus word
17. _____ bonus word

fold

Visual Memory

Fill in the missing letters. Write **ou** or **ow**.

1. t_____n

2. h_____se

3. gr_____p

4. f_____nd

5. foll_____

6. c_____sin

7. ab_____t

8. _____n

9. bel_____

10. w_____ld

11. ar_____nd

12. gr_____n

13. c_____ntry

14. sh_____ld

15. gr_____nd

Circle the 9 misspelled words in the paragraph.
Write them correctly on the lines.

My kussin went on a hike with a grup of children from toun.

They fallowed a path bello a small hill. They walked arownd

a grove of trees and saw a herd of cows resting on the groun.

Then it was time for everyone to go to my cuzin's howse for lunch.

_____   _____   _____

_____   _____   _____

_____   _____   _____

Word Meaning

Fill in the missing words.

1. The prairie dog _____ is under the _____.
   (below, town)   (country, ground)

2. My _____ lives in a _____ across the ocean.
   (cousin, group)   (country, around)

3. A large _____ of visitors stayed at our _____.
   (own, group)   (house, cousin)

4. The farmer's corn crop _____ be _____ by now.
   (around, should)   (own, grown)

5. Kelly looked all _____ trying to find her lost shoe.
   (around, ground)

6. Do you have your _____ computer at home?
   (town, own)

My Spelling Dictation

Write the sentences. Circle the spelling words.

1. _____

_____

_____

2. _____

_____

_____

86

Word Study

Listen for the vowel sounds.
Write the words in the correct boxes.

grown	group	ground	about	below
town	follow	would	own	should
found	country	around	cousin	house

sound of **o** in **go**	sound of **ow** in **cow**	sound of **oo** in **too**	sound of **u** in **up**	sound of **u** in **put**

Use words from the spelling list to make rhyming words.

1. shout _____

2. mouse _____

3. dozen _____

4. soup _____

5. could _____ _____

6. show _____ _____

7. ground _____ _____

8. bone _____

87

Building Spelling Skills

Spelling List

This Week's Focus:
- Review words with long vowel sounds
- Identify long vowels in open syllables

STEP 1 Read and Spell

STEP 2 Copy and Spell

STEP 3 Cover and Spell

fold

1. April
2. babies
3. over
4. hello
5. even
6. we
7. silent
8. tiny
9. menu
10. future
11. dear
12. raise
13. white
14. used
15. those
16. _____
   bonus word
17. _____
   bonus word

Match the parts to make words.
Write the words correctly on the lines.

1. A	ver	1. _April_
2. e	pril	2. _____
3. ba	ny	3. _____
4. si	u	4. _____
5. o	bies	5. _____
6. ti	ven	6. _____
7. men	lent	7. _____
8. fu	ture	8. _____

Circle the misspelled words.
Write the words correctly on the lines.

1. My grandmother says all babys are deer.

   _____   _____

2. Mr. Martin is going to raize tiney roses in his garden.

   _____   _____

3. It was sylent in the cave until someone yelled, "Heloo!"

   _____   _____

4. Last Aprul we painted our fence whyte.

   _____   _____

5. The teacher yousd thoze books in her class.

   _____   _____

Word Meaning

Answer the questions.

April	babies	over	hello	even
we	silent	tiny	menu	future
dear	raise	white	used	those

1. What do you use to choose a meal at a restaurant? _____

2. Which word means…?

    time that hasn't happened yet   _____

    above something   _____

    not new   _____

    a greeting   _____

    no sound   _____

3. How do you change the word **baby** to
    make it mean "more than one baby"?   _____

4. What month comes after March?   _____

My Spelling Dictation

Write the sentences. Circle the spelling words.

1. _____

    _____

    _____

2. _____

    _____

    _____

Word Study

Read the words. Listen for a long vowel sound.
Write the words in the correct boxes.

April	raised	used	over	babies
tiny	menu	those	silent	hello
we	white	future	even	

long **a**	long **o**	long **e**	long **i**	long **u**

An open syllable has a vowel at the end. The vowel is usually long.

Divide these words into syllables.
Circle the open syllable in each word.

1. April ___A___ ___pril___

2. babies _____ _____

3. over _____ _____

4. hello _____ _____

5. even _____ _____

6. lady _____ _____

7. silent _____ _____

8. tiny _____ _____

9. menu _____ _____

10. future _____ _____

Bonus: vacation _____ _____ _____

Spelling List

This Week's Focus:
- Spell words with the short **u** sound
- Spell words with the schwa sound
- Review words with long vowel sounds

STEP 1 Read and Spell

STEP 2 Copy and Spell

STEP 3 Cover and Spell

fold

1. disagree
2. again
3. given
4. other
5. money
6. problem
7. does
8. of
9. some
10. laid
11. change
12. tired
13. read
14. nice
15. lower
16. _____ bonus word
17. _____ bonus word

Find the words hiding in this puzzle.

a	g	a	i	n	c	h	a	n	g	e	p
l	a	i	d	p	r	o	n	i	o	x	r
o	o	s	v	o	u	t	t	c	c	f	o
w	m	o	n	e	y	h	r	e	a	d	b
e	e	m	g	q	n	e	b	y	n	o	l
r	h	e	e	t	i	r	e	d	t	e	e
a	g	d	i	s	a	g	r	e	e	s	m

again	nice
change	of
disagree	other
does	problem
given	read
laid	some
lower	tired
money	

Circle the 12 misspelled words.
Write them correctly on the lines.

Jack had a prblum yesterday. He wanted to red a good

book, so he went to a nyce bookstore. Jack picke out a book and

handed his muney to the clerk.

Jack said to the clerk, "This is not the write chanje."

The clerk counted the monny agin. Jack was rite. The clerk

gave him some more mony, and Jack went home to reed his book.

_____ _____ _____

_____ _____ _____

_____ _____ _____

_____ _____ _____

Word Meaning

Fill in the missing words.

again	change	disagree	does	given
laid	lower	money	nice	of
other	problem	read	some	tired

1. _____ Arthur have enough _____ to buy a ticket?

2. Did the _____ lady help you solve your _____?

3. I _____ with what I just _____ in the newspaper.

4. My hen _____ some _____ her eggs in the weeds behind the chicken coop.

5. Harry was _____ five dollars for cutting Mrs. Murphy's lawn.

6. Would you like to have _____ of my chocolate bar?

My Spelling Dictation

Write the sentences. Circle the spelling words.

1. _____

_____

_____

2. _____

_____

_____

Word Study

Underline the words that have the schwa sound.
Circle the letters that make the sound.

> (a)bout   less(o)n

1. disagree	6. tired	11. problem
2. again	7. given	12. used
3. lower	8. nice	13. silent
4. laid	9. read	14. those
5. change	10. raise	15. tiny

Fill in the blank with a rhyming spelling word.

> | other | money | read | laid |
> |---|---|---|---|
> | change | nice | tired | some |

1. arrange _____

2. fired _____

3. honey _____

4. paid _____

5. bread _____

6. twice _____

7. brother _____

8. drum _____

Spelling List

This Week's Focus:
- Spell words with the variant sounds of **g** and **c**

STEP 1 Read and Spell	STEP 2 Copy and Spell	STEP 3 Cover and Spell
1. city		
2. cereal		
3. face		
4. could		
5. guess		
6. huge		
7. age		
8. danger		
9. goose		
10. gone		
11. coast		
12. clean		
13. guard		
14. giant		
15. carton		
16. _____ bonus word		
17. _____ bonus word		

fold

Visual Memory

Find the words hiding in this puzzle.

```
c  e  r  e  a  l  a  g  e  d  o
g  i  g  u  a  r  d  o  m  a  c
u  o  t  c  a  r  t  o  n  n  o
e  x  n  y  c  e  r  s  h  g  u
s  s  e  e  f  a  c  e  u  e  l
s  a  n  g  i  a  n  t  g  r  d
c  o  a  s  t  q  c  l  e  a  n
```

age	face
carton	giant
cereal	gone
city	goose
clean	guard
coast	guess
could	huge
danger	

Circle the misspelled words.
Write them correctly on the lines.

1. age

2. cartun

3. sereal

4. citee

5. clean

6. koast

7. could

8. danjer

9. fase

10. giant

11. gawn

12. goose

13. gard

14. guess

15. huje

_____   _____   _____

_____   _____   _____

_____   _____   _____

Fill in the missing words.

coast	city	age	guess
danger	clean	guard	giant

1. The movie star had a _____ to protect her.

2. Have you ever been to New York _____?

3. The warning sign read "_____! Falling rocks."

4. The magician could _____ a person's _____.

5. Did you help _____ up the beach on Saturday?

6. Why does she always buy _____-sized packages of everything?

7. I can see sailboats off the _____.

My Spelling Dictation

Write the sentences. Circle the spelling words.

1. _____

_____

_____

2. _____

_____

_____

98

Word Study

The letters **c** and **g** make a hard and a soft sound.

Read each word and listen to the sound of the bolded letter.
Write it in the correct box.

age	**g**iant	**c**lean	**c**oast	fa**c**e
carton	**g**one	**g**uess	**c**ould	**g**oose
cereal	**c**ity	hu**g**e	dan**g**er	**g**uard

c		g	
hard /**k**/	soft /**s**/	hard /**g**/	soft /**j**/

Fill in the blanks with spelling words that mean the opposite.

1. country _____

2. tiny _____

3. safety _____

4. dirty _____

Fill in the missing spelling words and their opposites.

1. When faced with _____, he ran for _____.

2. The _____ goat hid from the _____ wolf.

3. He was _____ in class this morning, but is _____ now.

Building Spelling Skills

Spelling List

This Week's Focus:
- Spell r-controlled words with **or**, **er**, **ir**, **ur**, and **ear**

STEP 1 Read and Spell	STEP 2 Copy and Spell	STEP 3 Cover and Spell
1. word		
2. work		
3. world		
4. were		
5. first		
6. girl		
7. turned		
8. learn		
9. bird		
10. fire		
11. here		
12. nurse		
13. jury		
14. stirred		
15. wear		
16. _____ bonus word		
17. _____ bonus word		

fold

Unscramble the words. Write them on the lines.

word	were	turned	fire	jury
work	first	learn	here	stirred
world	girl	bird	nurse	wear

1. rowk _____

2. drow _____

3. gril _____

4. laern _____

5. fier _____

6. weer _____

7. nuser _____

8. brid _____

9. rowld _____

10. yurj _____

11. frist _____

12. raew _____

13. ternud _____

14. sterrid _____

15. reeh _____

Circle the 9 misspelled words.
Write them correctly on the lines.

Raul was on his way to wurk when he tirned a corner and saw a house on frie. Ferst, he called 911. Then, he looked around the house.

Raul herd a gril calling for help. He helped her crawl out a window.

At the hospital, a nurse took good care of the gerl. The child said, "I want to lurn how to be a nurs when I grow up."

_____ _____ _____

_____ _____ _____

_____ _____ _____

Word Meaning

Answer the questions.

word	work	world	were	first
girl	turned	learn	bird	fire
here	nurse	jury	stirred	wear

1. Who helps sick and injured people? _____

2. Which spelling word means...? the earth _____

   flames _____

   mixed it up _____

3. What do you call letters put together to represent something? _____

4. Who decides if a person is innocent or guilty of a crime? _____

5. Which spelling word is the opposite of ...?

   last _____   boy _____

   play _____   there _____

My Spelling Dictation

Write the sentences. Circle the spelling words.

1. _____

   _____

   _____

2. _____

   _____

Word Study

Circle the letters that make the /er/ sound in these words.

1. f i r s t　　　3. t u r n e d　　　5. w o r d　　　7. f a s t e r

2. l e a r n　　　4. g i r l　　　6. w e r e　　　8. w o r k

Fill in the missing letters to make spelling words. Write **er, ir, ur, ear,** or **or.**

1. n_____se　　　3. w_____e　　　5. l_____n　　　7. w_____d

2. b_____d　　　4. w_____ld　　　6. quick_____　　　8. st_____red

Write the spelling word that rhymes with each of these words.

word	work	world	were	first
girl	learn	fire	wear	nurse

1. care　_____　　4. burst　_____　　7. bird　_____

2. fur　_____　　5. curl　_____　　8. liar　_____

3. clerk　_____　　6. fern　_____　　9. purse　_____

Fill in the missing spelling words.

1. What are you going to _____ to the party?

2. Where _____ the boys going in such a hurry?

3. My dad has to _____ in the garden this Saturday.

4. Her mother is a _____ in Dr. Chan's office.

Spelling List

This Week's Focus:
- Spell r-controlled words with **ar**, **are**, **or**, and **ore**

STEP 1 Read and Spell	STEP 2 Copy and Spell	STEP 3 Cover and Spell

fold

1. aren't
2. partner
3. hard
4. chart
5. farm
6. start
7. large
8. more
9. before
10. horse
11. north
12. morning
13. care
14. stare
15. warning
16. _____
    bonus word
17. _____
    bonus word

Visual Memory

Match the parts to make a spelling word.
Write the complete word on the line.

1. far	th	1.	_farm_
2. lar	n't	2.	
3. nor	m	3.	
4. are	re	4.	
5. sta	ge	5.	
6. warn	fore	6.	
7. be	ner	7.	
8. part	ing	8.	

Circle the misspelled words.
Write them correctly on the lines.

1. arent	6. narth	11. hourse
2. care	7. stayr	12. partnur
3. mor	8. morning	13. hard
4. charte	9. befor	14. warning
5. farm	10. start	15. larje

_____ _____ _____

_____ _____ _____

Word Meaning

Fill in the missing words.

1. His _____ rode off _____ daybreak.
   (partner, start)   (horse, before)

2. Is it hard work to run a _____ _____?
   (care, large)   (more, farm)

3. We must _____ on our trip early in the _____.
   (start, warning)   (before, morning)

4. Read the _____ on the _____ before you dive in.
   (morning, warning)   (start, chart)

5. It isn't polite to _____ at people.
   (care, stare)

6. The explorer had a _____ trip going by dog sled.
   (north, hard)

My Spelling Dictation

Write the sentences. Circle the spelling words.

1. _____

   _____

   _____

2. _____

   _____

   _____

Word Study

Fill in the missing letters to make a spelling word.
Write **ar**, **or**, **are**, or **ore**.

1. p__ar__tner

2. n_____th

3. m_____ning

4. c_____

5. h_____d

6. _____en't

7. bef_____

8. w_____ning

9. st_____

10. l_____ge

11. m_____e

12. ch_____t

13. st_____t

14. h_____se

15. f_____m

Write the opposite of each word from your spelling list.

1. easy _____

2. tiny _____

3. less _____

4. after _____

5. south _____

6. evening _____

7. finish _____

Fill in the missing spelling words and their opposites.

1. The _____ giant and the _____ elf were friends.

2. I take a walk in the _____ and again in the _____.

3. Migrating birds fly _____ in the fall and _____ in the spring.

4. I do my homework _____ dinner, and then I play _____ dinner.

Building Spelling Skills

WEEK 23

Spelling List

This Week's Focus:
- Spell words with the vowel sounds in **to**, **top**, **wall**, and **up**
- Recognize homophones **threw** and **through**
- Spell words with suffixes -**less** and -**ful**

STEP 1 Read and Spell	STEP 2 Copy and Spell	STEP 3 Cover and Spell
1. threw		
2. through		
3. thoughtless		
4. caught		
5. fault		
6. taught		
7. because		
8. one		
9. once		
10. water		
11. watch		
12. wanted		
13. wonder		
14. wonderful		
15. walk		
16. _____ bonus word		
17. _____ bonus word		

fold

Visual Memory

Find the words hiding in this puzzle.

```
w a n t e d e d b e c
t h o u g h t l e s s
h r t a u g h t c w o
r e w a t e r o a o n
e w a a n d o o u n c
w f a u l t u n s d e
w a t c h k g w e e t
o n c a u g h t x r e
n w o n d e r f u l d
```

because	through
caught	walk
fault	wanted
once	watch
one	water
taught	wonder
thoughtless	wonderful
threw	

Circle the misspelled words.
Write them correctly on the lines.

1. wundir

2. caught

3. walk

4. wunce

5. becuz

6. tawght

7. thoughtless

8. watur

9. through

10. fawlt

11. wanted

12. throo

13. wach

14. onederful

15. one

_____   _____   _____

_____   _____   _____

_____   _____   _____

Word Meaning

Answer the questions.

threw	walk	one	through	wonderful
once	water	wonder	watch	thoughtless
caught	wanted	because	fault	taught

1. Which spelling words rhyme with ...?

   bought _____   _____

   new _____   _____

2. What does **watch** mean in this sentence? Circle your answer.
   You must watch your step when you climb a ladder.

   a. be careful   b. something that tells time   c. standing guard

3. Which word means "only one time"?   _____

4. What is the past tense of ...?

   catch _____   teach _____

   throw _____   want _____

My Spelling Dictation

Write the sentences. Circle the spelling words.

1. _____

   _____

   _____

2. _____

   _____

Word Study

Read the words. Listen for the vowel sounds.
Write each word in the correct box.

wanted	water	through	walk
threw	because	watch	taught
thought	caught	fault	

sound of **a** in **wall**	sound of **oo** in **too**

Add the correct suffix to the words.

(**-less** means "without")   (**-ful** means "filled with")

1. Morris had a _____ surprise.
   (wonder)

2. It was _____ of you to be late for the party.
   (thought)

3. The _____ man helped fix the flat tire.
   (thought)

4. I always feel _____ on my birthday.
   (joy)

5. A newborn kitten is _____.
   (help)

6. Will you be _____ and clean up that mess?
   (help)

Spelling List

This Week's Focus:
- Spell words that end with **or**, **ar**, and **er**
- Spell words with the final long **e** sound spelled **y**

STEP 1 Read and Spell

STEP 2 Copy and Spell

STEP 3 Cover and Spell

fold

1. color
2. odor
3. farmer
4. calendar
5. dollar
6. party
7. liar
8. after
9. number
10. better
11. doctor
12. weather
13. every
14. forty
15. sugar
16. _____ bonus word
17. _____ bonus word

Visual Memory

Match the parts. Write the words on the lines.

1. co	y	1. _color_
2. calen	ber	2. _____
3. part	lor	3. _____
4. ev	dar	4. _____
5. num	ery	5. _____
6. o	gar	6. _____
7. doc	dor	7. _____
8. for	tor	8. _____
9. su	ty	9. _____
10. weath	ter	10. _____
11. bet	er	11. _____

Circle the misspelled words. Write them correctly on the lines.

1. The calender cost one doller.

   _____   _____

2. Dad had a big partie when he turned fourty.

   _____   _____

3. You had bettir see the doctur about that bad cold.

   _____   _____

4. What nummer comes after nine?

   _____

5. Evry flower in the garden has a sweet oder.

   _____   _____

Word Meaning

Answer these questions.

color	odor	farmer	dollar	calendar
party	liar	after	number	better
doctor	weather	every	sugar	forty

1. Which letters make the /**er**/ sound in these words?

   liar _____   after _____   odor _____

2. What do you call someone who helps sick people?   _____

3. What do you call someone who is not truthful?   _____

4. Which spelling word has the /**sh**/ sound in **she**?   _____

5. Which spelling word means "all"?   _____

6. What is the opposite of...?

   before _____   worse _____

My Spelling Dictation

Write the sentences. Circle the spelling words.

1. _____

   _____

   _____

2. _____

   _____

   _____

Word Study

Underline all the words that have the /er/ sound in **her**.
Circle the letters that make the /er/ sound.

color   every   better

odor   calendar   sugar

party   watch   dollar

march   number   liar

weather   after   farmer

Divide the words into syllables.

1. color   col   or

2. calendar _____

3. better _____

4. dollar _____

5. farmer _____

6. number _____

7. party _____

8. liar _____

9. weather _____

10. odor _____

11. after _____

12. sugar _____

Spelling List

This Week's Focus:
- Spell words with the /f/ sound spelled **ph**, **gh**, and **f**
- Spell words with the base word **happy**
- Spell words with the suffixes **-ly** and **-ness**

STEP 1 Read and Spell	STEP 2 Copy and Spell	STEP 3 Cover and Spell

fold

1. phone

2. photograph

3. orphan

4. alphabet

5. graph

6. nephew

7. enough

8. father

9. half

10. Friday

11. cough

12. unhappy

13. happier

14. happily

15. happiness

16. _____
    bonus word

17. _____
    bonus word

Visual Memory

Match the parts to make a spelling word.
Write the complete word on the line.

1. Fri	phan		1. _____
2. fa	ew		2. _____
3. or	day		3. _____
4. neph	nough		4. _____
5. e	ther		5. _____
6. pho	hap	py	6. _____
7. al	to	bet	7. _____
8. un	pha	graph	8. _____

Circle the misspelled words.
Write them correctly on the lines.

1. fone   5. fotograph   9. orfan

2. haf   6. fadder   10. happiness

3. alfabet   7. nefew   11. enuf

4. cough   8. graph   12. Fritay

_____   _____   _____

_____   _____   _____

Word Meaning

Answer the questions.

phone	orphan	nephew	happiness	cough
alphabet	graph	enough	Friday	photograph
father	half	unhappy	happier	happily

1. What do you call a picture taken with a camera? _____

2. What is the word for a child with no parents? _____

3. What is a name for all the letters from **a** to **z**? _____

4. Which spelling word means "all that is needed"? _____

5. What do you do when you have a bad cold? _____

6. Which spelling words are names for family members?

_____ _____

My Spelling Dictation

Write the sentences. Circle the spelling words.

1. _____

_____

_____

2. _____

_____

Word Study

Sometimes the digraph **ph** and **gh** stand for the /**f**/ sound.
Fill in the missing letters. Write **f**, **ph**, or **gh**.

1. _ph_one

2. enou____

3. or____an

4. ____ather

5. ____riday

6. ne____ew

7. hal____

8. gra____

9. al____abet

10. ____otogra____

Fill in the missing letters to complete the spelling word.

1. Grandmother has an old ph_____ of her mother.

2. The first-grade teacher wrote the _____ph_____ on the chalkboard.

3. I ate _____f of the chicken on F_____.

A suffix is something you add to the end of words to change the meaning.
Change these words by adding a suffix.

(**ly** means "in this way")   (**ness** means "the state of being")

1. She climbed _____ and _____ up the ladder.
   (slow)   (careful)

2. The explorers were surrounded by _____ inside the cave.
   (dark)

3. Red Riding Hood skipped along _____ to Grandma's house.
   (happy)

4. His _____ filled my heart with _____.
   (kind)   (happy)

Spelling List

This Week's Focus:
- Spell words with silent letters
- Spell words with the prefixes **un-** and **re-**

STEP 1 Read and Spell	STEP 2 Copy and Spell	STEP 3 Cover and Spell

fold

1. ghost
2. neighbor
3. high
4. knew
5. knot
6. unknown
7. rewrap
8. wrong
9. written
10. wrapper
11. unwrap
12. climb
13. limb
14. gnaw
15. gnat
16. _____ bonus word
17. _____ bonus word

Visual Memory

Find the words hiding in this puzzle.

```
g  h  o  s  t  k  n  e  w  z
n  e  i  g  h  b  o  r  r  w
k  x  g  g  i  r  l  e  i  r
n  w  n  n  h  k  i  w  t  a
o  r  o  a  a  g  m  r  t  p
t  o  t  t  s  w  b  a  e  p
u  n  k  n  o  w  n  p  n  e
o  g  u  m  c  l  i  m  b  r
i  n  u  n  w  r  a  p  g  o
```

climb	neighbor
ghost	rewrap
gnat	unknown
gnaw	unwrap
high	wrapper
knew	written
knot	wrong
limb	

Circle the misspelled words.
Write them correctly on the lines.

1. gost
2. naybor
3. hi
4. gnat

5. knot
6. knoo
7. unknone
8. rewrap

9. rong
10. written
11. onwrap
12. clim

13. limb
14. naw

_____   _____   _____

_____   _____   _____

_____   _____   _____

15. The ribbon was tied in a not.   _____

16. Little nats flew around the fruit tree.   _____

17. A lim broke off the tree during the storm.   _____

Building Spelling Skills, Daily Practice • EMC 2707

Word Meaning

Complete the crossword puzzle.

Across
1. not known
4. to move up a ladder
6. to take off the covering
8. the spirit of someone dead seen by a person
9. a fastening made by tying string together

Down
2. a person who lives next door
3. the opposite of **right**
5. words were put on paper
7. a small insect
8. to chew on

ghost	high	gnaw	limb	knot
written	knew	unknown	unwrap	wrong
rewrap	climb	gnat	neighbor	

My Spelling Dictation

Write the sentences. Circle the spelling words.

1. _____

_____

_____

2. _____

_____

_____

Word Study

Read each word.
Mark an **X** over the silent letters.

̶w̶rap	̶knot

ghost	limb	knot	unwrap
high	knew	rewrap	climb
gnaw	write	wrong	gnat

Write the correct prefix in front of each word.

un means "not"	**re** means "again"
unhappy means "not happy"	**reread** means "read again"

1. My cat tore the paper on the gift, so Mother had to _____ it.
   (wrap)

2. The name of the artist was _____.
   (known)

3. People were _____ of what to do after the earthquake.
   (sure)

4. My homework paper was messy, so I had to _____ it.
   (write)

5. _____ the present to see what is inside.
   (Wrap)

6. Uncle Ted must _____ the fence every five years.
   (paint)

Spelling List

This Week's Focus:
• Spell words with the suffixes **-ful**, **-ly**, **-less**, **-er**, and **-est**

STEP 1 Read and Spell

fold

1. useful
2. quietly
3. slowly
4. careful
5. careless
6. quickly
7. useless
8. worthless
9. fearful
10. fearless
11. joyful
12. smarter
13. fastest
14. funniest
15. happiest
16. _____ bonus word
17. _____ bonus word

STEP 2 Copy and Spell

STEP 3 Cover and Spell

Visual Memory

Write the missing suffix to make a spelling word.

> ful   ly   less   er

1. use_ful_____

2. use_____

3. quiet_____

4. worth_____

5. smart_____

6. slow_____

7. joy_____

8. fast_____

9. care_____

10. care_____

11. fear_____

12. fear_____

Circle the misspelled words.
Write them correctly on the lines.

1. Mother walked slooly and kwietly past the sleeping baby.

   _____ _____

2. Carla was joyfull when she won the ribbon for fastist runner in school.

   _____ _____

3. It is useles to do the job if you are kareless.

   _____ _____

4. Pete is the happyest person I know.

   _____

5. A feerless shepherd quikly chased away the hungry wolf.

   _____ _____

Word Meaning

Answer the questions.

useful	quietly	slowly	careful	quickly
careless	useless	fearful	joyful	worthless
smarter	fastest	fearless	funniest	happiest

1. What do these words do?   **smarter**   **fastest**

   a. name something   b. compare something   c. describe something

2. What do these words do?   **thoughtless**   **useful**

   a. name something   b. compare something   c. describe something

3. Which spelling word is the opposite of ...?

   quickly _____   useful _____

   careless _____   saddest _____

4. Which word means "afraid"?   _____

My Spelling Dictation

Write the sentences. Circle the spelling words.

1. _____

   _____

   _____

2. _____

   _____

   _____

Word Study

Add the suffix **est** to these words.
Mark what you did to change the word.

	no change	double final consonant	change **y** to **i**
1. fast _fastest_	✔		
2. happy _____			
3. quick _____			
4. funny _____			
5. sad _____			
6. big _____			
7. smart _____			
8. silly _____			
9. small _____			

Add suffixes to the words to complete the sentences. Write **ful** or **less**.

1. Be care_____ as you work so you don't make a care_____ mistake.

2. The fear_____ firefighter rescued the fear_____ boy from the tree.

3. One sock is use_____, but two socks are use_____.

Spelling List

This Week's Focus:
- Spell words with the long **a**, long **e**, and short **e** sounds
- Spell words in the **-other**, **-ead**, **-eat**, and **-ear** word families
- Recognize the /**ur**/ sound in **heard** and **early**

STEP 1 Read and Spell

fold

1. brother
2. mother
3. another
4. field
5. friend
6. heard
7. early
8. friendly
9. head
10. near
11. year
12. shield
13. eat
14. measure
15. break
16. _____
   bonus word
17. _____
   bonus word

STEP 2 Copy and Spell

STEP 3 Cover and Spell

Visual Memory

Visual Memory

Find the words hiding in this puzzle.

```
m  e  a  s  u  r  e  e  a  a
o  n  e  h  e  a  r  d  n  n
t  r  y  i  e  l  f  s  o  b
h  x  n  e  n  d  i  e  t  r
e  e  e  l  a  h  e  a  h  e
r  a  a  d  o  r  l  r  e  a
n  t  r  d  e  a  d  l  r  k
f  r  i  e  n  d  l  y  o  r
a  n  o  b  r  o  t  h  e  r
```

another	head
break	heard
brother	measure
early	mother
eat	near
field	shield
friendly	year

Circle the misspelled words. Write them correctly on the lines.

1. My muther and bruther have the same birthday.

   _____ _____

2. Trina hurd from an old frend today.

   _____ _____

3. We herd a noise in the empty feeld next door.

   _____ _____

4. Erly next yeer they are moving to Texas.

   _____ _____

5. May I eta unother slice of pie?

   _____ _____

Word Meaning

Complete the crossword puzzle.

Across

1. close by
3. the opposite of **sister**
7. a female parent
10. a piece of armor
12. listened to
13. a person who knows and likes another person

Down

2. the opposite of **late**
4. to chew and swallow food
5. to find the size of something
6. the top part of your body
8. to smash
9. an open area with few trees
11. January 1 to December 31

break	brother	friend	field	near
head	heard	measure	year	
shield	mother	eat	early	

My Spelling Dictation

Write the sentences. Circle the spelling words.

1. _____

_____

_____

2. _____

_____

_____

Word Study

Read the words. Listen for the vowel sounds.
Write the words in the correct boxes.

eat	friend	break	measure
head	field	shield	

long **e**	long **a**	short **e**

Change the beginning sounds to create new words.

_____mother	_____ead	_____eat	_____ear
_____other	_____ead	_____eat	_____ear
_____other	_____ead	_____eat	_____ear
_____other	_____ead	_____eat	_____ear

Spelling List

This Week's Focus:
- Recognize homophones
- Review words with long vowel sounds

STEP 1 Read and Spell	STEP 2 Copy and Spell	STEP 3 Cover and Spell

fold

1. they're

2. there

3. their

4. soup

5. night

6. knight

7. right

8. write

9. weight

10. wait

11. piece

12. peace

13. hour

14. our

15. wrote

16. _____ bonus word

17. _____ bonus word

Visual Memory

Match the scrambled word to the correct spelling.

1. ecape	their	7. twai	right
2. ousp	soup	8. peice	wait
3. threi	there	9. rou	piece
4. heret	peace	10. hrou	wrote
5. ightn	write	11. ritgh	hour
6. ritwe	night	12. rwote	our

Circle the misspelled words. Write them correctly on the lines.

1. Their going to get they're books.

   _____ _____

2. The brave night saved a princess last nite.

   _____ _____

3. Mom said to weight here for an howr.

   _____ _____

4. Hour friends came to dinner last nitgh.

   _____ _____

5. May I have a peace of there pizza?

   _____ _____

6. Can you right a recipe for that soop?

   _____ _____

Word Meaning

Fill in the missing words.

1. Can you put _____ coats in the closet over _____?
   (their, there)   (they're, there)

2. The _____'s fight lasted all _____ long.
   (knight, night)   (knight, night)

3. Try to _____ the spelling word _____ this time.
   (right, write)   (right, write)

4. We spent an _____ with _____ grandfather.
   (our, hour)   (our, hour)

5. What is the _____ of that huge hog?
   (wait, weight)

6. That _____ of paper is a _____ treaty.
   (peace, piece)   (peace, piece)

My Spelling Dictation

Write the sentences. Circle the spelling words.

1. _____

   _____

   _____

2. _____

   _____

   _____

Word Study

Read the words. Listen for the vowel sounds.
Write the words in the correct boxes.
Circle the letters that spell the sounds.

wait	peace	night	right	piece	stare
write	weight	beach	stair	sight	plane
flee	knight	plain	beech	flea	site

long **a**	long **i**	long **e**
w(a)(i)t		

Write the opposite of each word from the spelling list.

1. erase _____   4. left _____

2. day _____   5. war _____

3. here _____   6. whole _____

Fill in the missing words.

1. If you _____ the word wrong, make it _____.

2. The generals signed the _____ treaty late one _____.

Spelling List

This Week's Focus:
- Review long and short vowel sounds
- Review how to divide words into syllables

STEP 1 Read and Spell	STEP 2 Copy and Spell	STEP 3 Cover and Spell

fold

1. air
2. against
3. all right
4. until
5. presents
6. beautiful
7. favorite
8. clothes
9. people
10. vacation
11. remember
12. already
13. hospital
14. minute
15. straight
16. _____ bonus word
17. _____ bonus word

Visual Memory

Match the parts to make spelling words.
Write the complete words on the lines.

1. a	ents		1. _____
2. un	ute		2. _____
3. pres	gainst		3. _____
4. peo	til		4. _____
5. min	ple		5. _____
6. beau	ca	ber	6. _____
7. va	read	ful	7. _____
8. re	ti	tal	8. _____
9. al	pi	y	9. _____
10. hos	mem	tion	10. _____

Circle the misspelled words.
Write them correctly on the lines.

1. air	6. bootiful	11. already
2. alright	7. favrute	12. remimber
3. strate	8. clothes	13. hospital
4. against	9. peeple	14. minite
5. presunts	10. vacashun	15. until

_____   _____   _____

_____   _____   _____

Word Meaning

Complete the crossword puzzle.

Down

1. a place for the care of the sick or injured
2. not crooked
3. very pretty
4. men, women, and children
5. men, women, and children
6. the one you like best

Across

4. gifts
7. a time of rest from school or work
8. what people wear
9. happened before this time
10. don't forget

| already | clothes | people | remember | hospital |
| beautiful | favorite | presents | straight | vacation |

My Spelling Dictation

Write the sentences. Circle the spelling words.

1. _____

_____

_____

2. _____

_____

_____

Word Study

Circle the letters in the words that make the given sound.

short u	until
short i	minute until
long i	all right
long o	clothes
long e	already remember
long a	favorite straight vacation

Divide the words into syllables.

1. against   _a   gainst_
2. presents   _____
3. beautiful   _____
4. favorite   _____
5. people   _____

6. vacation   _____
7. minute   _____
8. hospital   _____
9. already   _____
10. remember   _____

          Building Spelling Skills, Daily Practice • EMC 2707

Spelling Record Sheet

Building Spelling Skills

Students' Names															
1															
2															
3															
4															
5															
6															
7															
8															
9															
10															
11															
12															
13															
14															
15															
16															
17															
18															
19															
20															
21															
22															
23															
24															
25															
26															
27															
28															
29															
30															

Note: Reproduce this form twice for each student to track his or her progress.

My Spelling Record

Spelling List	Date	Number Correct	Words Missed

Spelling Test

Building Spelling Skills

Listen to the words.
Write each word on a line.

1. _____   10. _____

2. _____   11. _____

3. _____   12. _____

4. _____   13. _____

5. _____   14. _____

6. _____   15. _____

7. _____   16. _____

8. _____   17. _____

9. _____

Listen to the sentences.
Write them on the lines.

1. _____

_____

_____

2. _____

_____

_____

Building Spelling Skills

Spelling List
Note: Reproduce this form to make your own spelling list.

STEP 1 Read and Spell

STEP 2 Copy and Spell

STEP 3 Cover and Spell

fold

1. _____
2. _____
3. _____
4. _____
5. _____
6. _____
7. _____
8. _____
9. _____
10. _____
11. _____
12. _____
13. _____
14. _____
15. _____
16. _____
17. _____

Word Box

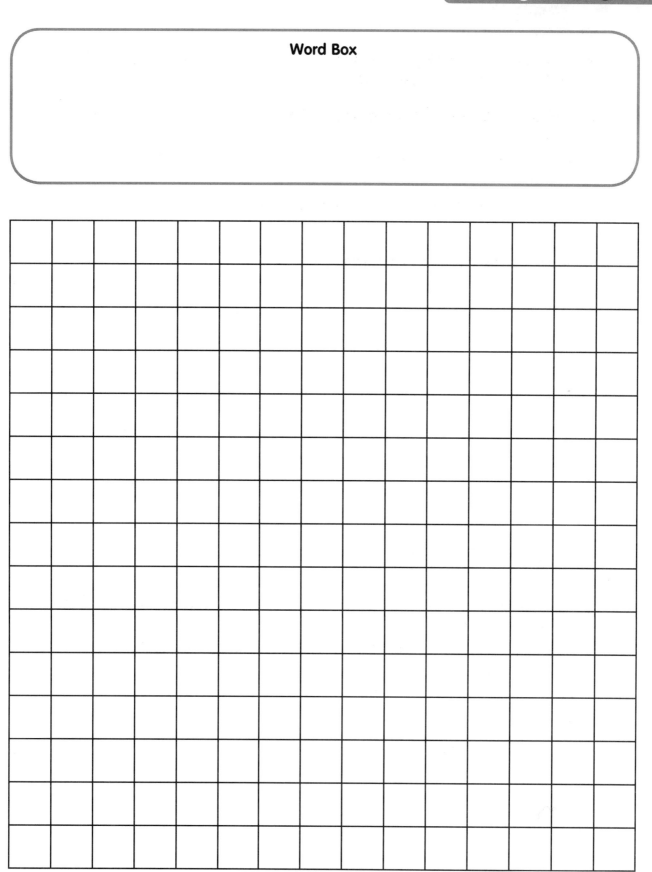

Building Spelling Skills

Dear Parents,

Attached is your child's spelling list for this week. Encourage him or her to practice the words in one or more of these ways:

1. Read and spell each word. Cover it up and write it. Uncover the word and check to see if it is correct.
2. Find the words on the spelling list in printed materials such as books and magazines.
3. Read a word aloud and ask your child to spell it (either aloud or written on paper).

Thank you for your support of our spelling program.

Sincerely,

- -

Building Spelling Skills

Dear Parents,

Attached is your child's spelling list for this week. Encourage him or her to practice the words in one or more of these ways:

1. Read and spell each word. Cover it up and write it. Uncover the word and check to see if it is correct.
2. Find the words on the spelling list in printed materials such as books and magazines.
3. Read a word aloud and ask your child to spell it (either aloud or written on paper).

Thank you for your support of our spelling program.

Sincerely,

Student Spelling Dictionaries

Self-made spelling dictionaries provide students with a reference for words they frequently use in their writing.

Materials

- copy of "My Own Spelling Dictionary" form (page 147)
- 26 sheets of lined paper—6" x 9" (15 x 23 cm)
- 2 sheets of construction paper or tagboard for cover—6" x 9" (15 x 23 cm)
- crayons or markers
- glue
- stapler
- masking tape

Steps to Follow

1 Color and cut out the cover sheet form. Glue it to the front cover of the dictionary.

2 Staple the lined paper inside the cover. Place masking tape over the staples.

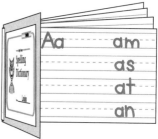

3 Guide students (or ask parent volunteers) to write a letter of the alphabet on each page.

What to Include

1. When students ask for the correct spelling of a special word, have them write it in their dictionary.

2. Include special words being learned as part of science or social studies units.

3. Include words for special holidays.

4. Include the common words students continue to misspell on tests and in daily written work.

5. Add color and number words if these are not on charts posted in the classroom.

My Own
Spelling
Dictionary

Name _____

- -

My Own
Spelling
Dictionary

Name _____

Master Word List

about	brook	didn't	float	help
above	brother	different	follow	here
added	brought	disagree	food	high
afraid	buy	do	football	hold
after	calendar	doctor	forty	homework
again	called	does	found	horse
against	came	doesn't	Friday	hospital
age	can't	doing	friend	hour
air	care	dollar	friendly	house
alike	careful	don't	fuel	huge
alive	careless	drawing	full	human
all right	carry	drink	funniest	I
almost	carton	due	future	I'll
along	catch	early	getting	I'm
alphabet	caught	earthquake	ghost	into
already	cereal	easy	giant	it's
also	change	eat	girl	its
always	chart	eight	give	joined
another	chew	ended	given	joked
April	children	enjoy	gnat	joyful
aren't	chocolate	enough	gnaw	jury
around	choice	even	gone	kind
ask	choose	every	good	knew
away	city	everybody	goose	knight
awful	clean	everyone	graph	knot
babies	climb	everywhere	great	know
balloon	close	eye	ground	ladies
basketball	clothes	face	group	lady
beautiful	coach	falling	grow	laid
because	coast	family	grown	large
become	coin	farm	guard	learn
been	color	farmer	guess	leave
before	coming	fastest	half	left
believe	cookie	father	happened	let's
below	cough	fault	happening	letter
better	could	favorite	happier	liar
between	country	fearful	happiest	life
bird	cousin	fearless	happily	light
blew	cried	few	happiness	limb
blue	cry	field	hard	live
both	cube	finally	have	longer
bought	cute	find	having	looked
boy	danger	finish	head	lower
brain	dear	fire	heard	loyal
break	destroy	first	hello	mall

many	over	shoes	their	voyage
maybe	own	short	there	wait
mean	oyster	should	these	walk
measure	partner	show	they	wanted
menu	party	shy	they're	warning
middle	pattern	silent	think	watch
might	peace	skateboard	those	water
minute	people	slowly	thoughtless	waved
missed	phone	small	three	way
Mississippi	photograph	smarter	threw	we
money	piece	smiled	throne	wear
more	pitch	smiling	through	weather
morning	playing	so	tiny	weight
most	please	some	tired	were
mother	pocket	something	to	we're
move	pointing	song	today	where
much	poison	soup	together	which
music	presents	spelling	told	while
my	pretty	stand	too	white
myself	prey	stare	touch	who
near	price	start	tough	whole
neighbor	problem	started	town	why
nephew	push	stayed	toys	willing
new	put	still	tried	with
next	quickly	stirred	true	without
nice	quietly	stood	truth	won't
niece	raise	story	try	wonder
night	reached	straight	turned	wonderful
north	read	straw	two	word
number	received	strongest	under	work
nurse	remember	studied	unhappy	world
o'clock	rewrap	study	uniform	worthless
odor	right	such	unit	would
of	rocket	sugar	unknown	wouldn't
off	room	sure	until	wrapper
often	rough	surprise	unwrap	write
oily	said	surprises	upon	written
once	save	swam	use	wrong
one	school	swim	used	wrote
only	sea	swimming	useful	year
open	search	takes	useless	you
orphan	seen	taught	usually	young
other	sew	teacher	vacation	your
our	she	than	very	you're
outside	shield	that's	voice	zipper

You are a SUPER SPELLER!

Super Speller

Name

Congratulations!!

Building Spelling Skills, Daily Practice • EMC 2707

Answer Key

Page 21

1. afraid   2. eight   3. away
4. ask   5. great   6. takes
7. than   8. said   9. always
10. they   11. catch   12. prey

These words should be crossed out:

1. sed   8. thay
2. eitgh   9. aks
3. grait   10. stend
4. drey   11. paling
5. catsh   12. taks
6. ufraid   13. fhan
7. wavd   14. uway

Page 22

1. eight, prey
2. takes, catch
3. always, afraid
4. They, playing
5. waved, said
6. stand, away

Page 23

waved   catch   away   takes   great
ask   eight   stand   said   they
always   afraid   prey   than   playing

1. played   playing
2. asked   asking
3. preyed   preying
4. painted   painting

1. waved   waving
2. smiled   smiling
3. skated   skating
4. baked   baking

Page 25

1. between or believe   2. leave
3. easy, many, or very
4. many, easy, or very
5. please   6. three   7. help
8. she   9. believe or between
10. very, many, or easy
11. seen   12. next

These words should be circled:

1. Plez   Please
2. eat   leave
3. eezy   easy
4. ben   been
5. betwene   between
6. belive   believe
7. miny   many
8. free   three

Page 26

1. three   4. between
2. sea   5. please
3. a. easy   6. believe
   b. left
   c. many
   d. leave
   e. help

Page 27

three   left   she
please   believe   many
very   been   seen
help   between   leave
easy   sea   next

1. very
2. many
3. please
4. sea, she, or three
5. help
6. she, sea, or three
7. seen or between
8. believe
9. three, she, or sea
10. between or seen

Page 29

1. while   7. which
2. buy or try   8. eye
3. light   9. drink
4. my   10. pitch
5. life   11. kind or find
6. swim   12. why

These words should be circled:

1. bie   lite   buy   light
2. Witch   drenk   Which   drink
3. Trie   pitch   Try   pitch
4. aye   swem   eye   swim
5. Eye   by   I   buy

Page 30

1. I, eye
2. Why, buy, drink
3. Which, light
4. while, pitch
5. my, try
6. kind, life

Page 31

life   drink   try
pitch   while   I
my   light   buy
eye   which   find
why   kind   swim

Answers will vary but could include:

ind	ile	ight	ink
find	mile	bright	rink
kind	file	light	wink
rind	while	might	pink
mind	smile	tight	link
blind	tile	sight	think
bind	pile	fight	drink

Page 33

1. pocket   2. almost   3. grow
4. open   5. often   6. coach   7. most
8. also   9. throne
10. hold, told, or both   11. rocket
12. sew

These words should be crossed out:

1. roket   7. koach
2. whold   8. allso
3. offen   9. opun
4. thone   10. groe
5. amolst   11. tole
6. bofh   12. sowe

Page 34

1. throne   4. so, sew
2. pocket   5. open
3. told, hold   6. rocket

Page 35

grow   hold   throne
rocket   so   pocket
told   also   sew
most   often   almost
both   coach   open

One syllable   **Two syllables**

1. grow   1. rocket
2. told   2. also
3. hold   3. often
4. so   4. pocket
5. sew   5. open
6. both   6. almost
7. coach
8. throne
9. most

Page 37

1. much   7. fuel
2. touch   8. under
3. use   9. such
4. you   10. human
5. unit   11. music
6. few   12. young

These words should be circled:

1. undar   under
2. noo   new
3. yer   your
4. kute   cute
5. tuch   touch
6. yung   young
7. fuo   few
8. moosic   music

Page 38

Pictures will vary but must reflect sentence meaning.

Page 39

use   such   few
young   music   under
your   you   unit
cute   much   new
fuel   human   touch

---

1. much, such, or touch
2. young
3. under
4. use
5. few, you, or new
6. cute
7. new or you
8. fuel
9. such, much, or touch
10. your

---

1. under, thunder
2. few, new
3. cute, flute

Page 41

too   alike   blew   know
blue   two   to   do
above   move   save   have
give   live   alive

These words should be circled:

1. tow   two
2. ulike   alike
3. blew   blue
4. no   know
5. hav   have
6. geve   give
7. too   to
8. Moov   Move

Page 42

1. two
2. too
3. to
4. blew
5. blue
6. know
7. no

Page 43

1. give   5. blow
2. move   6. do
3. live   7. has
4. know   8. save

---

1. moved
2. know
3. blew
4. saved

---

alive ———— different
alike ———— below
above ———— dead

Page 45

These words should be circled:

1. missed   5. different
2. balloon   6. pattern
3. pretty   7. carry
4. letter   8. zipper

Page 46

1. spelling
2. Mississippi
3. balloon
4. zipper
5. carry
6. letter
7. different or middle
8. pattern

Page 47

1. bal loon   7. zip per
2. spell ing   8. will ing
3. pret ty   9. mid dle
4. let ter   10. car ry
5. add ed   11. miss ing
6. pat tern   12. Mis sis sip pi

---

1. spelling   5. pattern
2. off   6. missed
3. still   7. different
4. middle   8. Mississippi

Page 49

1. mm   7. l
2. m   8. ll
3. tt   9. m
4. t   10. m
5. d   11. k
6. pp   12. v

1. swimming   6. happened
2. getting   7. happening
3. coming   8. joked
4. having   9. smiled
5. doing   10. came

1. started
2. received
3. smiling

Page 50

1. swam   5. coming
2. swimming   6. came
3. happening   7. smiled
4. happened   8. smiling

Page 51

1. joked   5. ended
2. swam   6. smiled
3. happened   7. received
4. came   8. started

1. swimming—double *m*
2. getting—double *t*
3. receiving—drop *e*
4. coming—drop *e*
5. having—drop *e*
6. doing—no change
7. smiling—drop *e*
8. ending—no change
9. happening—no change
10. starting—no change
11. joking—drop *e*

Page 53

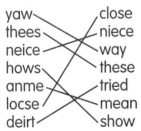

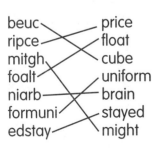

1. youniform   uniform
2. Cloze   Close
3. mite   might
4. kube   cube
5. staid   stayed
6. tryed   tried
7. shoo   show
8. flote   float

Page 54

Across	Down
1. mean	2. niece
4. price	3. brain
5. uniform	6. float
8. close	7. cube
9. these	10. stay

Page 55

1. way   a   8. close   o
2. these   e   9. tried   i
3. niece   e   10. cube   u
4. show   o   11. uniform   u
5. float   o   12. stayed   a
6. brain   a   13. price   i
7. mean   e

1. stayed—no change
2. tried—*y* to *i*
3. floated—no change
4. showed—no change
5. cried—*y* to *i*
6. hurried—*y* to *i*
7. planted—no change
8. worried—*y* to *i*
9. played—no change
10. scurried—*y* to *i*

Page 57

These words should be circled:

children   with   search
think   push   where
whole   sure   who
           teacher

These words should be circled:
1. Hoo   Who
   hole   whole
2. childrun   children
   poosh   push
3. finnish   finish
   shurt   short
4. tink   think
   serch   search
5. teecher   teacher
   togepher   together

Page 58

1. teacher, children
2. everywhere
3. think
4. finish
5. search
6. whole, short, together

Page 59

1. children   7. together
2. search   8. push
3. think   9. teacher
4. whole   10. with
5. where   11. short
6. finish   12. who

1. 3   6. 1   11. 1
2. 1   7. 1   12. 2
3. 1   8. 3   13. 1
4. 2   9. 1   14. 1
5. 1   10. 2   15. 1

Page 61

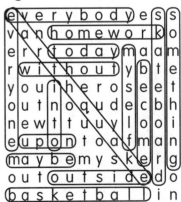

These words should be circled:

- homewerk — homework
- miself — myself
- owtside — outside
- skatbord — skateboard
- Everbody — Everybody
- baskutball — basketball
- Evrywon — Everyone
- sumthing — something
- erthquak — earthquake
- wifout — without

Page 62

1. basketball or skateboard
2. earthquake
3. homework, today
4. Something, into
5. upon
6. become
7. without
8. Everyone or Everybody, myself

Page 63

1. basketball
2. become
3. earthquake
4. everybody
5. everyone
6. homework
7. into
8. myself
9. maybe
10. outside
11. skateboard
12. something
13. today
14. upon
15. without

1. in|to
2. to|day
3. with|out
4. be|come
5. some|thing
6. may|be
7. out|side
8. home|work
9. earth|quake

Yes—Divide compound words into syllables between smaller words.

Page 65

1. awful
2. called
3. mall
4. song
5. small
6. along
7. rough
8. longer
9. straw
10. drawing
11. strongest
12. falling

These words should be circled:

1. ahful — awful
2. smal straw — small straw
3. drawn stronust — drawing strongest
4. bawght mol — bought mall
5. longa sog — longer song

Page 66

1. awful
2. straw
3. mall
4. drawing
5. bought   longer
   small   strongest
6. b

Page 67

awful   called   tough
mall   song   along
rough   bought   straw
strongest   falling   brought
small   drawing   longer

1. stronger   strongest
2. longer   longest
3. smaller   smallest
4. rougher   roughest
5. tougher   toughest

6. strongest
7. smaller
8. roughest
9. toughest
10. longer

Page 69

1. lady
2. family
3. only
4. surprises
5. ladies
6. study
7. finally
8. story
9. studied
10. surprise

These words should be circled:

1. suprise — surprise
2. shoos — shoes
3. cryed — cried
4. famuly — family
5. ladys — ladies
6. storie — story
7. finelly — finally
8. studyed — studied

Page 70

1. surprise
2. ladies
3. finally
4. study
5. surprises
6. cried

Page 71

y says i	y says e
cry	lady
shy	study
why	only
fly	story
my	family
try	funny

Note: Some children find the idea of dropping silent e before adding es confusing. You may choose to accept "add s" as correct answers for numbers 4 and 7.

1. ladies - y to i, add es
2. toys - add s
3. stories - y to i, add es
4. shoes - drop e, add es
5. families - y to i, add es
6. rockets - add s
7. nieces - drop e, add es

Page 73

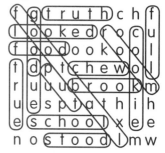

These words should be circled:

1. luked — looked
4. futbal — football
5. cookee — cookie
6. fud — food
8. poot — put
10. schol — school
12. doo — due
13. chu — chew
15. ruum — room

Page 74

Across	Down
1. food	1. full
3. football	2. cookie
7. brook	4. truth
9. chew	5. looked
10. good	6. true
	8. school

Page 75

u in **push**	o in **do**
looked	food
good	school
brook	truth
football	room
cookie	true
stood	chew
full	due
put	

1. full   4. put
2. good   5. truth
3. stood   6. true

Page 77

1. yoil — voice
2. cevoi — oily
3. soyter — boy
4. joyen — voyage
5. yob — oyster
6. agevoy — loyal
7. loyla — enjoy
8. ocin — coin
9. ingpoint — joined
10. cocholate — choice
11. edjoin — chocolate
12. oichce — pointing
13. sonpoi — destroy
14. troydes — poison

These words should be circled:
1. choyse — choice
   chocklate — chocolate
2. injoy — enjoy
   voyege — voyage
3. distroy — destroy
   poisen — poison
4. doy — boy
   oister — oyster
5. coyn — coin
   chose — choose

Page 78

1. oysters, voyage
2. Chocolate, choice
3. boy, destroy
4. pointing, coin
5. voice
6. poison

Page 79

1. boy	5. voice	9. destroy
2. oily	6. loyal	10. coin
3. choice	7. poison	11. enjoy
4. oyster	8. pointing	12. joined

1. points	pointed	pointing
2. joins	joined	joining
3. smiles	smiled	smiling
4. finishes	finished	finishing

1. smiling
2. points
3. finishes
4. joining

Page 81

1. don't	8. you're
2. didn't	9. we're
3. I'll	10. doesn't
4. that's	11. o'clock
5. it's	12. won't
6. can't	13. I'm
7. let's	14. wouldn't

These words should be circled:
1. din't — didn't
2. were — we're
3. duzn't — doesn't
4. Your — You're
5. Tat's — That's
6. Its — It's
7. kan't — can't
8. A'll — I'll

Page 82

Down	Across
1. can't	4. wouldn't
2. I'll	8. won't
3. doesn't	9. that's
4. don't	10. you're
6. o'clock	11. let's
7. it's	
8. we're	

Page 83

1. will not   do not
2. its
3. I'll

contractions	missing letters
1. don't	o
2. we're	a
3. they're	a
4. it's	i
5. wouldn't	o
6. can't	no
7. I'm	a
8. that's	i
9. doesn't	o
10. didn't	o
11. I'll	wi
12. let's	u

Page 85

1. town	6. cousin	11. around
2. house	7. about	12. grown
3. group	8. own	13. country
4. found	9. below	14. should
5. follow	10. would	15. ground

These words should be circled:
kussin — cousin
grup — group
toun — town
fallowed — followed
bello — below
arownd — around
groun — ground
cuzin's — cousin's
howse — house

Page 86

1. town, ground
2. cousin, country
3. group, house
4. should, grown
5. around
6. own

Page 87

o in **go**	ow in **cow**
grown	found
below	town
follow	about
own	ground
	house
	around

oo in **too**	u in **up**	u in **put**
group	country	would
	cousin	should

1. about
2. house
3. cousin
4. group
5. should   would
6. follow   below
7. around   found
8. own   grown

Page 89

1. A ———— ver   1. April
2. e ————— pril   2. even
3. ba ———— ny   3. babies
4. si ————— u   4. silent
5. o ————— bies   5. over
6. ti ————— ven   6. tiny
7. men ——— lent   7. menu
8. fu ———— ture   8. future

These words should be circled:
1. (babys) (deer) babies dear
2. (raize) (tiney) raise tiny
3. (sylent) (Heloo) silent Hello
4. (Aprul) (whyte) April white
5. (yousd) (thoze) used those

Page 90

1. menu
2. future
   over
   used
   hello
   silent
3. change the *y* to *i* and add *es*
4. April

Page 91

long **a**	long **o**	long **e**
raised	over	even
April	those	we
babies	hello	tiny
		babies

long **i**	long **u**
silent	used
white	future
tiny	menu

1. (A) pril   6. (la) dy
2. (ba) bies   7. (si) lent
3. (o) ver   8. (ti) ny
4. hel (o)   9. men (u)
5. (e) ven   10. (fu) ture
Bonus: (va) (co) tion

Page 93

a g a i n c h a n g e p
l a i d p r o n i o x r
o o s v o u t t c c f o
w m o n e y h r e a d b
e e m g a n e b y n o l
r h e e t i r e d t e e
a g d i s a g r e e s m

These words should be circled:
(prblum) problem
(red) read
(nyce) nice
(picke) picked
(muney) money
(write) right
(chanje) change
(monny) money
(agin) again
(rite) right
(mony) money
(reed) read

Page 94

1. Does, money
2. nice or other, problem
3. disagree, read
4. laid, of
5. given
6. some

Page 95

1. dis(a)gree   6. tired   11. prob(l)em
2. (a)gain   7. giv(e)n   12. used
3. lower   8. nice   13. sil(e)nt
4. laid   9. read   14. those
5. change   10. raise   15. tiny

1. change   5. read
2. tired   6. nice
3. money   7. other
4. laid   8. some

Page 97

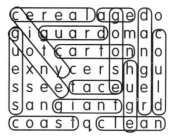

c e r e a l a g e d o
g i g u a r d o m a c
u o t c a r t o n n o
e x n y c e r s h g u
s s e e f a c e u e l
s a n g i a n t g r d
c o a s t q c l e a n

These words should be circled:
2. (cartun)   carton
3. (sereal)   cereal
4. (citee)   city
6. (koast)   coast
8. (danjer)   danger
9. (fase)   face
11. (gawn)   gone
13. (gard)   guard
15. (huje)   huge

Page 98

1. guard
2. City
3. Danger
4. guess, age
5. clean
6. giant
7. coast

Page 99

k	s	g	j
carton	cereal	gone	age
clean	city	goose	danger
coast	face	guard	giant
could		guess	huge

1. city   3. danger
2. huge or giant   4. clean

1. danger, safety
2. tiny, huge or giant
3. present, gone

Page 101

1. work	6. were	11. first
2. word	7. nurse	12. wear
3. girl	8. bird	13. turned
4. learn	9. world	14. stirred
5. fire	10. jury	15. here

These words should be circled:

wurk	work
tirned	turned
frie	fire
ferst	First
herd	heard
gril	girl
gerl	girl
lurn	learn
nurs	nurse

Page 102

1. nurse
2. world
   fire
   stirred
3. word
4. jury
5. first   girl
   work   here

Page 103

1. first   5. word
2. learn   6. were
3. turned   7. faster
4. girl   8. work

1. nurse   5. learn
2. bird   6. quicker
3. were   7. word
4. world   8. stirred

1. wear   4. first   7. word
2. were   5. girl   8. fire
3. work   6. learn   9. nurse

1. wear
2. were
3. work
4. nurse

Page 105

1. far — th
2. lar — n't
3. nor — m
4. are — re
5. sta — ge
6. warn — fore
7. be — ner
8. part — ing

1. farm
2. large
3. north
4. aren't
5. stare
6. warning
7. before
8. partner

These words should be circled:

1. arent	aren't
3. mor	more
4. charte	chart
6. narth	north
7. stayr	stare
9. befor	before
11. hourse	horse
12. partnur	partner
15. larje	large

Page 106

1. partner, before
2. large, farm
3. start, morning
4. warning, chart
5. stare
6. hard

Page 107

1. partner	6. aren't	11. more
2. north	7. before	12. chart
3. morning	8. warning	13. start
4. care	9. stare	14. horse
5. hard	10. large	15. farm

1. hard   5. north
2. large   6. morning
3. more   7. start
4. before

1. large, tiny
2. morning, evening
3. south, north
4. before, after

Page 109

These words should be circled:

1. wundr	wonder
4. wunce	once
5. becuz	because
6. tawght	taught
8. watur	water
10. fawlt	fault
12. throo	threw or through
13. wach	watch
14. onederful	wonderful

Page 110

1. caught   taught
   threw   through
2. a
3. once
4. caught   taught
   threw   wanted

Page 111

a in **wall**	oo in **too**
thought	threw
because	through
caught	
fault	
taught	
wanted	
water	
watch	
walk	

1. wonderful
2. thoughtless
3. thoughtful
4. joyful
5. helpless
6. helpful

Page 113

1. co
2. calen
3. part
4. ev
5. num
6. o
7. doc
8. for
9. su
10. weath
11. bet

y · ber · lor · dar · ery · gar · dor · tor · ty · ter · er

1. color
2. calendar
3. party
4. every
5. number
6. odor
7. doctor
8. forty
9. sugar
10. weather
11. better

These words should be circled:

1. calender — calendar
   doller — dollar
2. partie — party
   fourty — forty
3. bettir — better
   doctur — doctor
4. nummer — number
5. Evry — Every
   oder — odor

Page 114

1. liar __ar__   after __er__   odor __or__
2. doctor
3. liar
4. sugar
5. every
6. after   better

Page 115

color   every   better
odor   calendar   sugar
party   watch   dollar
march   number   liar
weather   after   farmer

1. col or   7. par ty
2. cal en dar   8. li ar
3. bet ter   9. weath er
4. dol lar   10. o dor
5. farm er   11. af ter
6. num ber   12. sug ar

Page 117

1. Fri
2. fa
3. or
4. neph
5. e
6. pho
7. al
8. un

phan · ew · day · nough · ther · hap — py · to · bet · pha · graph

1. Friday   5. enough
2. father   6. photograph
3. orphan   7. alphabet
4. nephew   8. unhappy

These words should be circled:

1. fone — phone
2. haf — half
3. alfabet — alphabet
5. fotograph — photograph
6. fadder — father
7. nefew — nephew
9. orfan — orphan
11. enuf — enough
12. Friday — Friday

Page 118

1. photograph
2. orphan
3. alphabet
4. enough
5. cough
6. father, nephew

Page 119

1. phone   6. nephew
2. enough   7. half
3. orphan   8. graph
4. father   9. alphabet
5. Friday   10. photograph

1. photograph
2. alphabet
3. half, Friday

1. slowly, carefully
2. darkness
3. happily
4. kindness, happiness

Page 121

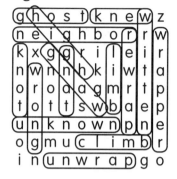

These words should be circled:

1. gost — ghost
2. naybor — neighbor
3. hi — high
6. knoo — knew
7. unknone — unknown
9. rong — wrong
11. onwrap — unwrap
12. clim — climb
14. naw — gnaw
15. not — knot
16. nats — gnats
17. lim — limb

Page 122

Across   **Down**
1. unknown   2. neighbor
4. climb   3. wrong
6. unwrap   5. written
8. ghost   7. gnat
9. knot   8. gnaw

Page 123

ghost   limb   knot   unwrap
high   knew   rewrap   climb
gnaw   write   wrong   gnat

1. rewrap
2. unknown
3. unsure
4. rewrite
5. Unwrap
6. repaint

Page 125

1. useful	7. joyful
2. useless	8. fastest
3. quietly	9. careful
4. worthless	10. careless
5. smarter	11. fearful
6. slowly	12. fearless

These words should be circled:

1. slooly — slowly
   kwietly — quietly
2. joyfull — joyful
   fastist — fastest
3. useles — useless
   kareless — careless
4. happyest — happiest
5. feerless — fearless
   quikly — quickly

Page 126

1. b
2. c
3. slowly   useless
   careful   happiest
4. fearful

Page 127

1. fastest—no change
2. happiest—y to i
3. quickest—no change
4. funniest—y to i
5. saddest—double consonant
6. biggest—double consonant
7. smartest—no change
8. silliest—y to i
9. smallest—no change

1. careful, careless
2. fearless, fearful
3. useless, useful

Page 129

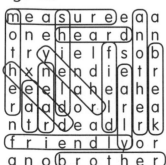

Page 130

These words should be circled:

1. muther, bruther — mother, brother
2. hurd, frend — heard, friend
3. herd, feeld — heard, field
4. Erly, yeer — Early, year
5. eta, anuther — eat, another

Page 130

Across	Down
1. near	2. early
3. brother	4. eat
7. mother	5. measure
10. shield	6. head
12. heard	8. break
13. friend	9. field
	11. year

Page 131

long **e**	long **a**	short **e**
eat	break	head
field		measure
shield		friend

Answers will vary but may include:

other	dead	eat	ear
mother	read	beat	hear
brother	head	seat	near
another	lead	neat	year
smother	thread	wheat	fear

Page 133

1. ecape — their
2. ousp — soup
3. threi — there
4. heret — peace
5. ightn — write
6. ritwe — night
7. twai — right
8. peice — wait
9. rou — piece
10. hrou — wrote
11. ritgh — hour
12. rwote — our

These words should be circled:

1. Their, They're — They're, their
2. night, nite — knight, night
3. weight, howr — wait, hour
4. Hour, nitgh — Our, night
5. peace, there — piece, their
6. right, soop — write, soup

Page 134

1. their, there
2. knight's, night
3. write, right
4. hour, our
5. weight
6. piece, peace

Page 135

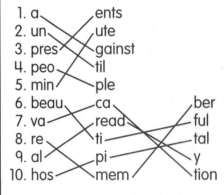

1. write	4. right
2. night	5. peace
3. there	6. piece

1. write, right
2. peace, night

Page 137

1. a — ents
2. un — ute
3. pres — gainst
4. peo — til
5. min — ple
6. beau — ca — ber
7. va — read — ful
8. re — ti — tal
9. al — pi — y
10. hos — mem — tion

1. against
2. until
3. presents
4. people
5. minute
6. beautiful
7. vacation
8. remember
9. already
10. hospital

These words should be circled:

2. (alright)   all right
3. (strate)   straight
5. (presunts)   presents
6. (bootiful)   beautiful
7. (favrute)   favorite
9. (peeple)   people
10. (vacashun)   vacation
12. (remimber)   remember
14. (minite)   minute

Page 138

Down
1. hospital
2. straight
3. beautiful
5. people
6. favorite

Across
4. presents
7. vacation
8. clothes
9. already
10. remember

Page 139

short **u**—(u)ntil
short **i**—m(i)nute   unt(i)l
long **i**—all r(igh)t
long **o**—cl(o)thes
long **e**—alread(y)   r(e)member
long **a**—f(a)vorite   str(aigh)t   v(aca)tion

1. a gainst
2. pres ents
3. beau ti ful
4. fa vor ite
5. peo ple
6. va ca tion
7. min ute
8. hos pi tal
9. al read y
10. re mem ber